To:

Breanna

Happy 18th

From:

Uncle Gerry
& Aunt Patty

365 Devotions to Inspire Your Day

hugs™

Daily
Inspirations
Words of
Promise

HOWARD BOOKS
A DIVISION OF SIMON & SCHUSTER
New York   London   Toronto   Sydney

Our purpose at Howard Books is to:
- *Increase faith* in the hearts of growing Christians
- *Inspire holiness* in the lives of believers
- *Instill hope* in the hearts of struggling people everywhere

Because He's coming again!

HOWARD
BOOKS

Published by Howard Books, a division of Simon & Schuster, Inc.
1230 Avenue of the Americas, New York, NY 10020
www.howardpublishing.com

Hugs Daily Inspirations: Words of Promise © 2007 by Howard Books

ISBN 13: 978-1-4165-4178-3
ISBN 10:   1-4165-4178-0

11 10 9 8 7 6 5 4 3 2

HOWARD and colophon are registered trademarks of Simon & Schuster, Inc.

Manufactured in China

For information regarding special discounts for bulk purchases, please contact Simon & Schuster Special Sales at 1-800-456-6798 or business@simonandschuster.com.

Compiled by Criswell Freeman
Edited by Between the Lines
Cover design by Stephanie D. Walker
Interior design by Bart Dawson

The stars may fall,
but God's promises
will stand and be fulfilled.

—J. I. Packer

Introduction

God has made many promises to you, promises that can be found in a book like no other: the Bible. The Bible is both an invaluable gift from above and a practical tool for everyday living. But sometimes, amid the demands and challenges of life, we can lose sight of the blessings and assurances contained in God's Word. This book is intended as an easy-to-use refresher course about the things God can do in your heart and life—and the things He can do through you.

These 365 devotions focus on God's promises, God's plan, God's instructions, and God's love. Perhaps you've heard about these topics, in one form or another, on many occasions. But it never hurts to be reminded. So throughout the coming year, try this simple experiment: read one page in this guide each day. If you've already established the habit of spending a few quiet moments each morning with God, this book will enrich your experience. If not, you'll discover that by turning your attention to spiritual matters, even briefly, you can set a positive direction of your day and improve the quality of your life.

Each day brings with it opportunities to give yourself an emotional hug by reaffirming your trust in a loving, faithful Creator. When you trust Him, you'll also worship Him—not just with words but with deeds. And as you learn to trust your heavenly Father completely and to follow Him faithfully, you'll discover that God always keeps His promises. Always!

January

God's Promises

Let's keep a firm grip on the promises
that keep us going. He always keeps his word.
Hebrews 10:23 MSG

God's Word contains promises upon which you can and should depend, promises that address every aspect of your life.

Are you tired? Discouraged? Fearful? Trust the assurances God has made to you. Are you worried or anxious? Be confident in God's power. Do you see a difficult future ahead? Rely upon your Creator for help and support. Are you confused? Listen to the quiet voice of your heavenly Father. He is not a God of confusion.

Talk to God; listen to Him; trust Him, and trust His promises. Get a firm grip on them and hold on tight, knowing that God always keeps His word.

We have ample evidence
that the Lord is able to guide. The promises cover
every imaginable situation. All we need to do is
to take the hand He stretches out.
Elisabeth Elliot

The Promise of Abundance

*I have come that they may have life,
and that they may have it more abundantly.*
John 10:10 NKJV

When the Bible describes God's promise of the abundant life, is it talking about the acquisition of material riches or earthly fame? Actually, it's talking about something even better. When God's Word promises that we can experience abundance, it's describing a higher spiritual plane, an elevated level of emotional maturity, a sense of genuine security that gives meaning and richness to life.

All of us are free to accept God's gifts or to reject them; that choice, and the consequences that follow, are ours and ours alone. How we choose determines how we live.

Today and every day, you are surrounded by God's blessings; it's up to you to recognize them and to embrace them. Open your mind and your heart to God's riches. Then share those riches with a world in desperate need of the God kind of abundance.

*God is the giver, and we are the receivers.
And His richest gifts are bestowed not upon those who
do the greatest things, but upon those who accept His
abundance and His grace.*
Hannah Whitall Smith

A Book Filled with Promises

*Man does not live on bread alone,
but on every word that comes from the mouth of God.*
Matthew 4:4 NIV

God's promises are found in a book like no other—the Bible is one of the most important tools God uses to direct our steps and transform our lives. As you seek to build a deeper relationship with your Creator, you can use His promises as a light for your path and a guide for your steps.

If you read your Bible often—and if you trust the promises that you find there—you will be blessed. When you study God's Word, you'll find new meaning and fresh perspective, even from the most familiar passages. When you live according to its principles, you'll find joy and fulfillment.

So consider your Bible a gift from above, a tool for improving your day and your life . . . because that's precisely what it is.

*God gives us a compass and a Book of promises
and principles—the Bible—and lets us make our decisions
day by day as we sense the leading
of His Spirit. This is how we grow.*
Warren Wiersbe

The Rewards of Integrity

The integrity of the upright guides them,
but the unfaithful are destroyed by their duplicity.
Proverbs 11:3 NIV

The Bible promises that God rewards integrity just as surely as He punishes duplicity. So when we make integrity the hallmark of our dealings with others, we can look forward to a surprising array of blessings—blessings God bestows on those who trust His Word and honor His commandments.

Integrity is established slowly over a lifetime, but it's lived out moment by moment. Integrity is the sum of every right decision, every honest word, every noble thought, and every heartfelt prayer. It is built upon a foundation of industry, generosity, and humility. A character of integrity is a precious thing—difficult to build but easy to tear down. We must seek to live each day with discipline, honesty, and faith. When we do, integrity becomes a habit. And God smiles.

There's nothing like the power of integrity.
It is a characteristic so radiant, so steady,
so consistent, so beautiful, that it makes
a permanent picture in our minds.
Franklin Graham

Real Contentment

I have learned to be content
in whatever circumstances I am.
Philippians 4:11 HCSB

Where can you find contentment? Is it a result of wealth, power, beauty, fame? No, genuine contentment springs from a peaceful spirit, a clear conscience, and a loving heart—like yours!

Our world seems preoccupied with the search for happiness. We're bombarded with messages telling us that happiness hinges on the acquisition of material possessions. But those messages are false. Contentment is not the result of what we own; it is the result of our disposition.

The search for contentment is an internal quest, an exploration of the heart, the mind, and the soul in relation to the Creator. You can find contentment—indeed you will find it—if you simply look in the right place. When you trust God's promises and place your life in His hands, you'll at last find real contentment.

The secret of contentment in the midst of change
is found in having roots in the changeless Christ—the same
yesterday, today and forever.
Ed Young

If You Become Discouraged

*Do not be afraid or discouraged, for the Lord will
personally go ahead of you. He will be with you;
he will neither fail you nor abandon you.*
Deuteronomy 31:8 NLT

Even the most optimistic people can become
discouraged as they go through the ups and
downs of life. Ours is a world where demands and
expectations can seem almost impossibly high.
When you feel you're not measuring up—or if you're
convinced that you're being treated unfairly—it's easy
to become disheartened.

But when you encounter difficult circumstances,
don't lose hope. When you face uncertainties about
the future, don't become anxious. And if you become
discouraged, don't despair. Instead, trust God's
promises as you lift your thoughts and your prayers
to Him. When you do, He will go before you and
guide you—and knowing that He will never fail you is
the best medicine for dissolving discouragement.

*The most profane word we use is hopeless.
When you say a situation or person is hopeless,
you are slamming the door in the face of God.*
Kathy Troccoli

God's Promise of Strength

*Those who hope in the LORD will renew their strength.
They will soar on wings like eagles; they will run
and not grow weary, they will walk and not be faint.*
Isaiah 40:31 NIV

All of us have moments when we feel exhausted. We all suffer through tough times, difficult days, and perplexing periods in our lives. Yet even in the midst of trouble, there's good news: God promises to give us comfort and strength if we turn to Him.

If you're trying to meet too many demands and have too few hours in which to meet them, perhaps it's time to review your priorities and pare down your daily to-do list. Take time to focus on God and His love for you. Ask Him for the wisdom in prioritizing your life and strength to fulfill your responsibilities. God will give you the energy you need for your most important tasks . . . just put your hope in Him.

*No matter how heavy the burden, daily strength
is given, so I expect we need not give ourselves
any concern as to what the outcome will be.
We must simply go forward.*
Annie Armstrong

New Beginnings

> *Do not remember the former things,*
> *nor consider the things of old.*
> *Behold, I will do a new thing.*
> Isaiah 43:18–19 NKJV

Each new day is filled with opportunities: opportunities to seek God's will, opportunities to serve God's children, and opportunities to improve your own life and the lives of your loved ones. Your twofold challenge is to look for these opportunities and to seize them.

Don't dwell on what happened yesterday. Consider this day a new beginning, a fresh start, an open door to serving your Creator with willing hands and a loving heart. Ask God to renew your sense of purpose as He guides your steps, and ask Him to help you invest your talents wisely.

God has created this day and given it to you with the promise of a new beginning. Embrace it and make the most of it!

> *Whatever you can do, or dream you can,*
> *begin it. Boldness has genius,*
> *power, and magic in it.*
> Goethe

Expect a Miracle

With men it is impossible, but not with God,
because all things are possible with God.
Mark 10:27 HCSB

God promises that all things are possible with Him, and He promises to work good things in the lives of those who trust Him. Count yourself among that number today and every day of your life.

When you put your faith in God, you avail yourself of His power and His peace. And when you take God at His word—when you believe that absolutely nothing is impossible for Him—you'll be amazed at the things He can do.

Today, as you fulfill the responsibilities of everyday life, expect God to do big things for you and yours. Trust that the Creator of the universe is capable of moving any mountain, including the ones looming ahead of you. And don't ever be afraid to ask for a miracle . . . because God is a miracle-working God.

For every mountain there is a miracle.
Robert Schuller

Never Distant

Do not be afraid or discouraged.
For the Lord your God is with you wherever you go.
Joshua 1:9 NLT

God has promised that He will be with us wherever we go. He is never absent from our lives or from our world; to the contrary, God's hand is actively involved in not just the big events but also the smallest details of everyday life. He is not somewhere "out there"; He is right here, right now, working in your world . . . and in you.

God is with you always, listening to your thoughts and prayers, watching your every step. When the burdens of life weigh down upon you, you may be tempted to ignore God, or so distracted that you don't sense His presence. But if you'll quiet yourself and spend time with Him, God will comfort your heart and restore your spirit.

At this very moment, God is seeking to work in you and through you. Are you willing to let Him?

God's presence is with you, but you
have to make a choice to believe—and
I mean, really believe—that this is true.
This conscious decision is yours alone.
Bill Hybels

Just Do It

*Do what God's teaching says; when you only listen
and do nothing, you are fooling yourselves.*
James 1:22 NCV

If you've acquired the habit of doing your most important work first (even if you'd rather be doing something else), congratulations! But if you find yourself putting off unpleasant tasks until later (or never), you might want to give some thought to the consequences of that behavior.

Chronic procrastinators squeeze the joy out of their own lives. It can be difficult to summon the determination, courage, and wisdom to overcome procrastination. But you can free yourself from emotional quicksand by paying less attention to your fears and more attention to your responsibilities—they're really opportunities, you know. So when you're faced with a difficult choice or an unpleasant task, don't waste time fretting over your fate. Simply seek God's counsel and get busy. When you do, you will be richly rewarded because of your willingness to act.

*Forward, then. Forward! Let us go forward without fear
into the future, and let us dread not when duty calls.*
Winston Churchill

God's Amazing Plans for You

*No one has ever imagined what God has prepared
for those who love him.*
1 Corinthians 2:9 NCV

God has big plans for your life—wonderful, even surprising plans. But He will not force those plans on you. It's up to you to tune your heart and your mind to God's intentions, even when the world pressures you to do otherwise.

Each day you wake up to a world overflowing with time-wasting distractions and life-devouring temptations. Your challenge is to avoid these pitfalls. How? By focusing on the talents God has given you, and by using those talents to pursue the opportunities He places along your path.

God wants to use you in wonderful, unexpected ways. Will you let Him? When you do, you'll be amazed at the creativity and the beauty of His plan for you.

*God has no problems, only plans.
There is never panic in heaven.*
Corrie ten Boom

God's Armor

Be strong in the Lord and in his mighty power.
Put on the full armor of God so that you can
take your stand against the devil's schemes.
Ephesians 6:10–11 NIV

In a world filled with dangers and temptations, God is the ultimate armor. In a world filled with misleading messages, God's Word is the ultimate truth. In a world filled with more frustrations than we can count, God offers the ultimate peace. Will you accept God's peace and wear God's armor against the dangers of our world?

Sometimes, in the crush of everyday life, God may seem far away; but He's not. God is everywhere you have ever been and everywhere you will ever go. He is with you night and day; He knows your thoughts and hears your prayers. He is your powerful protector. And when you stand strong in Him, you can count on His help and protection in the battles you face today.

Prayer is our pathway not only to
divine protection, but also to a personal,
intimate relationship with God.
Shirley Dobson

Hope for Today and Forever

*I have told you these things so that in Me
you may have peace. In the world you have suffering.
But take courage! I have conquered the world.*
John 16:33 HCSB

Despite God's promises, despite His love, and despite our countless blessings, we frail human beings can still lose hope from time to time. When we do, we need the encouragement of thoughtful friends, the life-changing power of prayer, and the healing truth of God's Word.

If you find yourself falling into the spiritual traps of worry and discouragement, remember the hopeful words of John 16:33. In this passage Jesus offers the assurance of peace and hope—peace for today and hope for the future.

This world can be a place of trials and tribulations, but when we trust God's promises and hold tightly to the hope we have in Him, we can feel secure. God has promised us peace, joy, and eternal life. And God keeps His promises today, tomorrow, and forever.

*God is the only one who can make the valley of trouble a
door of hope.*
Catherine Marshall

The Joy God Promises

I am coming to You, and I speak these things in the world
so that they may have My joy completed in them.
John 17:13 HCSB

God intends for you to share His joy. Yet sometimes, amid the hustle and bustle of life, we sometimes forfeit—even if only temporarily—the Father's joy as we wrestle with the challenges of daily living.

When God promises that you can experience His abundance and His peace, do you believe Him? You should. After all, God keeps every one of His promises—no exceptions.

So here's a prescription for better spiritual health: Learn to trust God, and open the door of your soul to Him. Expect to experience His joy. Treat this day, and every day, as a priceless opportunity and a cause for celebration. When you do, God will give you the peace and joy He has promised.

Where the soul is full of peace and joy,
outward surroundings and circumstances
are of comparatively little account.
Hannah Whitall Smith

True Love

Love is patient, love is kind and is not jealous; love does not brag and is not arrogant, does not act unbecomingly; it does not seek its own, is not provoked, does not take into account a wrong suffered, does not rejoice in unrighteousness, but rejoices with the truth; bears all things, believes all things, hopes all things, endures all things.
1 Corinthians 13:4–7 NASB

True love is more than a feeling—it is a decision to do what's required to make love last through good times and hard times. Genuine love is inevitably translated into acts of kindness, both large and small. Real love is patient, understanding, consistent, and considerate. Love is an endurance race, a journey that requires ample servings of faith and forgiveness.

God wants more for you than mediocre relationships; He created you to give and to receive true love. Yes, real love requires effort, but God will equip you for that work, because He knows that the fruits of your labor will enrich not only your life but also the lives of your loved ones and generations yet unborn.

Sacrificial love, giving-up love, is love that is willing to go to any lengths to provide for the well-being of the beloved.
Ed Young

Passion and Purpose

May He grant you according to your heart's desire,
and fulfill all your purpose.
Psalm 20:4 NKJV

We all need to discover a purpose for our lives, a purpose that excites us and causes us to live each day with passion.

Author Anna Quindlen had this advice: "Consider the lilies of the field. Look at the fuzz on a baby's ear. Read in the backyard with the sun on your face. Learn to be happy. And think of life as a terminal illness, because, if you do, you will live it with joy and passion, as it ought to be lived."

If you have not yet discovered a passionate pursuit that blesses you and your world, don't give up. Keep searching, and keep trusting that with God's help, you can and will find a meaningful way to live—serving your neighbors and your Creator—with passion and purpose.

When we wholeheartedly commit ourselves to God, there is
nothing mediocre or run-of-the-mill
about us. To live for Christ is to be passionate
about our Lord and about our lives.
Jim Gallery

Finding Inner Peace

I leave you peace; my peace I give you.
I do not give it to you as the world does.
So don't let your hearts be troubled or afraid.
John 14:27 NCV

Are you at peace with the direction of your life? Or are you still rushing after the illusion of "peace and happiness" that the world promises but cannot deliver? The answer to this simple question will have a dramatic impact on your life.

Lasting peace begins and ends with God: with His promises, with His love, with His security, and with His Son. Are you troubled or afraid? Weary of the world's empty promises? Real, lasting peace can be yours. But only God can give it.

Today, as a gift to yourself, to your family, and to your friends, accept God's gift of inner peace. It is offered freely; it is yours for the asking; it is part of God's plan for your life.

The happiness for which our souls ache is one undisturbed by success or failure, one which will root deeply inside us and give inward relaxation, peace, and contentment, no matter what the surface problems may be. That kind of happiness stands in need of no outward stimulus.
Billy Graham

Pleasing God

*Everything that goes into a life of pleasing God has been
miraculously given to us by getting to know,
personally and intimately, the One who invited us to God.
The best invitation we ever received!*
2 Peter 1:3 MSG

When God created you, he equipped you with an assortment of talents and abilities that are uniquely yours. It's up to you to develop those talents and to use them—in the unique way God created you to do so. But at times society will attempt to pigeonhole you, to standardize you, and to make you fit into a preformed mold. And at times, because you're an imperfect human being, you may become so wrapped up in meeting society's expectations that you fail to focus on God's expectations.

But what God has in store for you is infinitely better than any other alternative.

Whom will you try to please today: God or society? Your primary goal should not be to please imperfect men and women. To reach your full potential, strive diligently to please your all-knowing and gracious God.

*It is impossible to please God doing things motivated by
and produced by the flesh.*
Bill Bright

Trusting God's Answers

*Trust in the LORD with all your heart;
do not depend on your own understanding.*
Proverbs 3:5 NLT

God answers our prayers. What God does not do is this: He does not always answer our prayers as soon as we might like, and He does not always answer our prayers by saying yes to whatever we want. God isn't an order taker, and He's not some sort of cosmic vending machine. Sometimes—even when we want something desperately—our loving, heavenly Father responds to our requests by saying no. When He does, we must accept His answer, even if we don't understand it, knowing that He wants only the best for us.

God answers prayers not only according to our wishes but also according to His master plan. We cannot know that plan, but we can know the Planner . . . and we can trust His wisdom, His righteousness, and His love.

*I must often be glad that certain past prayers
of my own were not granted.*
C. S. Lewis

Renewal and Celebration

> *Behold, I am making all things new.*
> Revelation 21:5 NASB

Each new day offers countless opportunities to celebrate life and to serve God's children. But each day also offers many opportunities to fall prey to the distractions of our age.

Ours is a society brimming with distractions that threaten to distance us from God. In response to these distractions, our challenge is straightforward: we should focus on God's promises, on His will for our lives, and on His blessings. When we do, our everyday duties will become a cause for celebration. And when we trust God to lead us and guide us, He will renew us, just as the psalmist said in the familiar words of Psalm 23.

So today, honor your Creator by making your life a celebration. After all, your talents are unique, as are your opportunities. So the best time to really live—and really celebrate—is now.

> *Like a spring of pure water, God's peace in*
> *our hearts brings cleansing and refreshment*
> *to our minds and bodies.*
> Billy Graham

Silence and Peace

My soul, wait in silence for God only,
for my hope is from Him.
Psalm 62:5 NASB

Here in the noisy twenty-first century, silence is underrated. Many of us can't even seem to walk from the front door to the street without a cell phone or earbuds to our ears. The world seems to grow louder day by day, our senses overloaded or outright assaulted at every turn. But if we allow this clamor to drown out God's voice and His peace, we do ourselves a profound disservice. So if we're wise, we'll make time each day for quiet reflection.

Do you take time each day for a period of silence? And during those precious moments, do you sincerely open your heart to your Creator? If you do, you will be blessed, because that quiet time will enable you to immerse yourself more fully in the hope and peace found only in God's presence.

The remedy for distractions is the same now as it was in earlier and simpler times: prayer, meditation, and the cultivation of the inner life.
A. W. Tozer

Peace and Prayer

Watch therefore, and pray always.
Luke 21:36 NKJV

Do you seek a more peaceful life? Then you must lead a prayerful life. Do you have questions you can't answer? Ask your Father in heaven for guidance. Do you sincerely desire the gift of everlasting love and eternal life? God promises these gifts through His grace, and He waits with open arms and an open heart for you to accept.

When you weave the habit of prayer into the fabric of your day, you invite God to become a partner in every facet of your life. When you consult God on a consistent basis, you avail yourself of His wisdom, His strength, and His love. Your petitions to Him will transform you and will extend His blessings to your family and your world.

Today, turn everything over to your Creator in prayer. He is listening, and He wants to hear from you.

Don't be overwhelmed.
Take it one day and one prayer at a time.
Stormie Omartian

The Quality of Our Thoughts

*May the words of my mouth and the meditation
of my heart be pleasing to you, O LORD,
my rock and my redeemer.*
Psalm 19:14 NLT

Do you pay careful attention to the quality of your thoughts? Are you careful to direct those thoughts toward topics that are uplifting, enlightening, and pleasing to God? If so, congratulations. But if you find that your thoughts are hijacked from time to time by the negativity that pervades our troubled world, you're not alone. Much of society seems to focus on—and often glamorize—the negative aspects of life, and that's unfortunate.

God wants you to experience His joy and abundance. So today, enter into that joy and abundance by focusing your thoughts on those things that are worthy of praise (check out Philippians 4:8). Count your blessings instead of your hardships. When you do, you'll gladly offer words of thanks to your heavenly Father for His many wonderful gifts.

*If you want to know whether you're thinking correctly,
check it out in the Word.*
Charles Stanley

Acceptance

People may make plans in their minds,
but the LORD decides what they will do.
Proverbs 16:9 NCV

Sometimes we must accept life on its terms, not our own. Life has a way of unfolding not as we will but as it will. And sometimes there's precious little we can do to change things.

When events transpire that are beyond our control, we have a choice: we can either learn the art of acceptance, or we can make ourselves miserable as we struggle to change the unchangeable.

We must entrust the things we cannot change to God. Once we have done so, we can prayerfully and faithfully tackle the important work He has placed before us: doing something about the things we *can* change . . . with His help.

Once we accept our limits, we go beyond them.
Brendan Francis Behan

Ask Him

Ask in my name, according to my will,
and he'll most certainly give it to you.
Your joy will be a river overflowing its banks!
John 16:24 MSG

God offers us gifts, and we should accept them—yet often we don't. Why? Because we fail to trust our heavenly Father completely and because we are, at times, rather inflexible. God has plans for us, but sometimes we resist; and when we do, we pay a price for our shortsightedness.

In John 16:24, God promises that when we ask for things in His name, He will respond. He won't withhold His gifts when we ask for them, but ask for them we must. And if we're wise, we'll ask for them expectantly and often.

Are you a person who asks God to move mountains in your life, or are you expecting Him to stumble over molehills? Whatever the size of your needs, God can meet them; whatever the size of your obstacles, He can help you overcome them. Ask for His help today.

It is our part to seek, His to grant what we ask;
our part to make a beginning, His to bring it to
completion; our part to offer what we can,
His to finish what we cannot.
Saint Jerome

Faith or Fear

I may walk through valleys as dark as death,
but I won't be afraid. You are with me,
and your shepherd's rod makes me feel safe.
Psalm 23:4 CEV

Although God has probably guided you through many struggles and more than a few difficult days, you may still find your faith stretched to the limit when you encounter adversity, uncertainty, or unwelcome changes. But the good news is this: even though your circumstances may change, God's love for you does not.

The next time you're in a fear-inducing situation, remember that no problem is too big for the Good Shepherd. Meditate on the scope of God's power and His love, walk closely with Him, and let Him guide you through the changes in your life.

Wherever you are, God is there, too. He cares for you today and always, and He will lovingly accompany and protect you as you walk through life's shadowy valleys. And soon you'll find that your faith is stronger than your fear.

In a higher world it is otherwise; but here below,
to live is to change, and to be perfect
is to have changed often.
John Henry Cardinal Newman

Going to the House of the Lord

I was glad when they said to me,
"Let us go to the house of the LORD."
Psalm 122:1 NLT

The Bible teaches that we should worship God in our hearts and in our churches. We have clear instructions to "feed the church of God" (Acts 20:28 KJV) and that He will be there in the presence of fellow believers (Matthew 18:20).

But we live in a world that is teeming with temptations and distractions—a world where good and evil wage a constant battle for our minds, our hearts, and our souls. Our challenge is to ensure that we cast our lot on God's side. One way we remain faithful to Him is through the practice of regular, purposeful corporate worship. When we gather together and worship the Father faithfully and fervently, we will be blessed . . . and we'll be glad we spent time in the house of the Lord.

The church is not an end in itself;
it is a means to the end of the kingdom of God.
E. Stanley Jones

Making the Right Choices

I will make you wise and show you where to go.
I will guide you and watch over you.
Psalm 32:8 NCV

Are you facing a tough decision that has you confused? If so, here's a simple formula for making the right choice: let God decide. Instead of fretting about your future, pray about it.

When you consult your heavenly Father, you'll discover that He keeps His promises; and one of the things He's promised is that He will lead and guide you. So when you go to Him with your dilemma, that's precisely what He will do. When you spend time in His presence, listening to His voice, God will quietly lead you along a path of His choosing—a path that is right for you.

The next time you arrive at one of life's crossroads, consult God's road map (the Bible) and seek God's guidance (in prayer). When you do, you'll never stay lost for long.

As we trust God to give us wisdom for today's decisions,
He will lead us a step at a time into
what He wants us to be doing in the future.
Theodore Epp

Opportunities to Encourage

Encourage each other and give each other strength.
1 Thessalonians 5:11 NCV

During a typical day, how many opportunities will you have to encourage other human beings? Unless you're living on a deserted island, the answer is, "A lot!" Now here's a follow-up question: how often do you take advantage of those opportunities? It's a question each individual must answer for himself or herself; but those who live according to God's instructions in the Bible should be able to say, "More often than not."

Whether you realize it or not, you're surrounded by people who need an encouraging word, a helping hand, or a pat on the back. And every time you encourage one of these folks, you'll be doing God's will by obeying His Word. So today, be alert to opportunities to encourage others. You'll find that the strength you give them will find its way back to you.

When we bring sunshine into the lives of others, we're
warmed by it ourselves. When we spill
a little happiness, it splashes on us.
Barbara Johnson

Mountain-Moving Faith

I assure you: If anyone says to this mountain,
"Be lifted up and thrown into the sea," and does not
doubt in his heart, but believes that what he says
will happen, it will be done for him.
Mark 11:23 HCSB

Have you ever felt your faith in God slipping away? If so, you are not alone. Life is a series of successes and failures, celebrations and disappointments, joys and sorrows. But even when we feel down and our faith reserves feel empty, we can feed our faith by remembering that God is with us and that He works mightily on our behalf.

Jesus taught His disciples that if they had faith, they could move mountains. You can, too. When you place your faith, your trust, your life in God's hands, you'll be amazed at the marvelous things He can do with you and through you. So strengthen your faith through praise, through worship, through Bible study, and through prayer. And trust God's plans. With Him, all things are possible, and He stands ready to open a world of possibilities to you if you have faith.

Only God can move mountains,
but faith and prayer can move God.
E. M. Bounds

February

Sowing and Reaping

Remember this: the person who sows sparingly
will also reap sparingly, and the person who sows
generously will also reap generously.
2 Corinthians 9:6 HCSB

Would you like to reap a bountiful harvest?
Well, the Bible contains this promise: if you
sow generously, you'll reap generously as well. In
other words, if you want to be successful, you should
expect to work hard.

God has created a world in which hard work is
rewarded and little work returns little benefit. So you
should always assume that you'll need to invest some
quantity—and quality—of work to achieve the success
you desire.

Today presents an opportunity for you to do just
that: sow seeds (work) that will produce a harvest
(reward). The present is always a good time to plant
such seeds, but no one else will do it for you. So if
you want to reap the promised bountiful harvest,
start planting generously today.

"They that sow bountifully shall reap
also bountifully," is as true in spiritual things
as in material.
Lottie Moon

Being Generous

Freely you have received, freely give.
Matthew 10:8 NKJV

God's Word instructs us to be generous, compassionate servants to those who need our support. Because we have been richly blessed by our Creator, we, in turn, are called to share our gifts, our possessions, our talents, and our time.

Concentration-camp survivor Corrie ten Boom correctly observed, "The measure of a life is not its duration but its donation." These words remind us that the quality of our lives is determined not by what we receive from others but by what we share with others.

The thread of generosity is woven into the very fabric of Jesus's teachings. If we wish to follow His example, we, too, must be cheerful, generous, courageous givers. We should serve with smiles on our faces and empathy in our hearts. And it doesn't hurt to remember that when we bless others, we, too, will be richly blessed.

Giving from a grateful heart and expecting nothing in return is a sweet offering to the One who owns everything I have anyway. It's the very least I can do. And as I give, I experience God's grace.
Mary Hunt

Seeking His Kingdom

*Seek first the kingdom of God and His righteousness,
and all these things shall be added to you.*
Matthew 6:33 NKJV

A righteous life has many components: faith, honesty, generosity, love, kindness, humility, gratitude, and worship, to name but a few. If we hope to please God, we must live according to His guidelines. We must, to the best of our abilities, live according to the principles contained in God's Word.

The Bible contains thorough instructions which, if followed, lead to fulfillment, righteousness, and eternal life. But if we choose to disregard God's instructions, the results are as predictable as they are tragic.

So today, seek God's kingdom and follow His leading. Trust God's promises, and live in accordance with His Word. There's no better way to live.

*Our progress in holiness depends on God
and ourselves—on God's grace
and on our will to be holy.*
Mother Teresa

Critical Reflections

The Lord is gracious and compassionate,
slow to anger and great in faithful love.
Psalm 145:8 HCSB

God loves you. But what are you telling yourself about yourself? When you look in the mirror, are you staring back at your biggest cheerleader or your harshest critic? If you can learn to give yourself the benefit of the doubt—if you can learn how to have constructive conversations with the person you see in the mirror—then your self-respect will tend to take care of itself. But if you're constantly berating yourself—if you're constantly telling yourself that you can't measure up—then you'll find that self-respect is always in short supply.

The next time you find yourself being critical of the person you see in the mirror, think for a moment about God's love for you, and then ask yourself if the criticism is really valid. If it is valid, make changes . . . if not, lighten up.

Have patience with all things, but mostly with yourself.
Don't lose courage considering your own imperfections,
but instantly begin remedying them.
Every day begin the task anew.
Saint Francis de Sales

Following God's Plan

The counsel of the LORD stands forever,
the plans of His heart from generation to generation.
Psalm 33:11 NASB

Y ou can expect a satisfying and fulfilling existence when you follow God's plan for your life. But how can you discern God's will? You can begin by studying God's Word and obeying His commandments. Watch carefully for the signposts He places along your path, and be sure to associate with people who encourage your spiritual growth. Listen carefully to the still small voice of the Spirit that speaks to you in the quiet moments of your daily devotional time, and even throughout your day.

God wants to use you in wonderful ways, and He will if you let Him; but the decision to seek and follow God's plan is yours and yours alone. Today, choose to follow God's plan. Then you can look forward to receiving all the wonderful promises that come with a life lived for Him.

The joy of anything, from a blade of grass upwards,
is to fulfill its created purpose.
Oswald Chambers

Who Gets the Credit

Humble yourselves before the Lord, and He will exalt you.
James 4:10 HCSB

When we experience success, it's easy to proclaim, "I did that!" But as German theologian Dietrich Bonhoeffer once observed, "It is very easy to overestimate the importance of our own achievements in comparison with what we owe others." In other words, we are imperfect human beings who sometimes like to inflate our accomplishments.

Who are the greatest among us? Are they the proud and the powerful? Hardly. The greatest among us are the humble servants who care little for their own glory and much for God's glory. If we seek greatness in God's eyes, we must praise His good works, not our own.

If you're tempted to overestimate your own accomplishments, resist that temptation. Instead, give credit where credit is due, starting with God. There's really no such thing as a self-made man. All of us are made by God . . . and He deserves the credit and the glory, not us.

Humility is the only true wisdom
by which we prepare our minds for all
the possible changes of life.
George Arliss

Laughter as the Fountain of Youth

A merry heart makes a cheerful countenance.
Proverbs 15:13 NKJV

Laughter is good for the soul, so if you'd like a proven formula for maintaining a youthful countenance, here it is: laugh as often as you can.

Since life is brief, we owe it to ourselves and our loved ones to enjoy all the laughs we can. After all, hearty laughter is health food for the mind and medicine for the heart. Perhaps that's why so few sounds on earth can rival the happy reverberations of friends and family laughing together.

So do yourself this favor: acquire the habit of looking at the humorous side of life. When you do, you'll discover that, whatever your age, a good laugh can make you feel just a little bit younger.

A good laugh is sunshine in the house.
William Makepeace Thackeray

Forgiveness Day by Day

See to it that no one repays evil for evil to anyone,
but always pursue what is good for one another and for all.
1 Thessalonians 5:15 HCSB

God promises that when we forgive other people, we, too, will be forgiven (Matthew 6:14-15). But sometimes it's hard to forgive folks, especially the people who have hurt us badly.

If you're trapped in the emotional quicksand of bitterness, call on God to pull you out. Spend time talking to your heavenly Father, and ask Him specifically to lift the burdens of the past from your heart.

Each new day is a gift from above, but if your heart is filled with regret or anger, you won't be able to fully enjoy God's blessings. So if you're struggling to forgive someone who has hurt you, spend a few quiet moments each morning asking God to soften your heart. God can heal you—and He will—when you practice forgiveness and seek Him day by day.

Forgiveness is the key that unlocks
the door of resentment and the handcuffs of hate.
It is a power that breaks
the chains of bitterness and the shackles of selfishness.
Corrie ten Boom

The Marathon of Life

Since we also have such a large cloud of witnesses
surrounding us, let us lay aside every weight
and the sin that so easily ensnares us,
and run with endurance the race that lies before us.
Hebrews 12:1 HCSB

A well-lived life is like a marathon, not a sprint—it calls for preparation, determination, and lots of perseverance. As an example of perfect perseverance, we need look no further than Jesus of Nazareth.

Jesus finished what He began. Despite His suffering, despite the shame of the cross, Jesus was steadfast in His faithfulness to the Father. We, too, must remain faithful, especially during times of hardship. Sometimes our prayers may seem to meet with silence, and in those times we must patiently persevere, trusting that God is indeed listening and working in our lives.

Are you facing a difficult time in your life? Don't give up. Even though you're weary, run the race of life with endurance. Whatever your current problem, God can handle it. Your job is to persevere until He does.

When you fall and skin your knees
and skin your heart, He'll pick you up.
Charles Stanley

Spiritual Traps

Why are you cast down, O my soul?
And why are you disquieted within me?
Hope in God, for I shall yet praise Him for
the help of His countenance.
Psalm 42:5 NKJV

Sometimes, despite our trust in God's promises, we may fall into the spiritual traps of worry, frustration, or discouragement, and our hearts become heavy. What we need at such times is plenty of rest, a large dose of perspective, and God's healing touch. He is our Helper, and we can place our hope in Him without fear of disappointment.

Today, vow to be a hope-filled believer. Entrust all your cares to God, and think optimistically about your life, your family, your profession, and your future. Nurture your hopes, not your fears. Take time to meditate on God's goodness and faithfulness. Then, when you've filled your heart with hope and gladness, share your optimism with others. They'll be better for it . . . and so will you.

A pessimist is one who makes difficulties of
his opportunities; an optimist is one who makes
opportunities of his difficulties.
Harry S. Truman

Living on Purpose

*It is God who works in you to will and to act
according to his good purpose.*
Philippians 2:13 NIV

Life is best lived on purpose. And purpose, like everything else in the universe, begins with God. Whether you realize it or not, God has a plan for your life: a divine calling, a direction in which He is leading you. When you welcome God into your heart and establish a genuine relationship with Him, He will begin to make known—one step at a time—His purposes for you.

Sometimes God's intentions will seem crystal clear; other times, your understanding of His plan will seem incomplete at best. But even on those difficult days when you are unsure which way to turn, never lose sight of these truths: God created you for a reason; He has important work for you to do; and He's waiting patiently for you to do it. Step out in faith, and live a life of purpose.

I beg you do not squander life.
And don't live for this world only.
Billy Graham

Seeking God

You will seek me and find me
when you seek me with all your heart.
Jeremiah 29:13 NIV

When we seek God with open hearts and sincere prayers, God promises that we will find Him. And we need not look far, because He is with us always.

Sometimes, in the crush of our daily duties, God may seem far away; but He is not. God is everywhere we have ever been and everywhere we will ever go. He is with us night and day; He knows our thoughts and our prayers. And when we earnestly seek Him, we will find Him—because He's right here, just waiting for us to reach out to Him.

Today, reach out to the Giver of all blessings. Turn to Him for guidance and for strength. Invite God into every aspect of your life. And remember that no matter what your circumstances, God never leaves you; He is here, and He wants you to find Him.

Seeking after God is a two-pronged endeavor.
It requires not only humility to say,
"God, I need you," but also a heart that
desires a pure life that is pleasing to the Lord.
Jim Cymbala

Simply Rich

A simple life in the Fear-of-God
is better than a rich life with a ton of headaches.
Proverbs 15:16 MSG

Is yours a life of moderation or accumulation? Are you more interested in the possessions you can acquire or in the person you can become? The answers to these questions will go a long way in setting your direction for this day and, in time, the direction of your life.

In our affluent society, countless people and corporations vie for your attention, for your time, and for your dollars. Don't let them succeed in complicating your life! Keep your eyes—and your life—focused on God.

If your material possessions are somehow distancing you from your heavenly Father, discard them. If your outside interests leave you too little time for your family or your faith, slow down the merry-go-round—or better yet, get off the merry-go-round completely. Is your life full of headaches? Get back to the simple yet abundant life only God can offer, and you'll find those headaches melting away.

A man is rich in proportion to the number of things
he can afford to leave alone.
Henry David Thoreau

A World of Temptation

Look straight ahead, and fix your eyes on what lies
before you. Mark out a straight path for your feet;
stay on the safe path. Don't get sidetracked;
keep your feet from following evil.
Proverbs 4:25–27 NLT

Have you noticed that this world is filled to the brim with temptations? Unless you've been living the life of a hermit, you've noticed that enticements are everywhere.

With so much available in these modern times, it seems there's a steady stream of delectable-yet-dangerous delights, temptations that can cause pain and heartache in more ways than ever before. But in the battle against the dangers of this world, we are never alone. God is always with us, and He will give us the power to resist temptation when we ask Him for the strength to do so.

The apostle Peter offered this stern warning: "Your adversary the devil walks about like a roaring lion, seeking whom he may devour" (1 Peter 5:8 NKJV). We must take that warning seriously, and keep our feet on the straight and narrow path. When we do, God has promised to walk with us.

Do not fight the temptation in detail. Turn from it.
Look only at your Lord. Sing. Read. Work.
Amy Carmichael

A Day to Be Glad

This is the day the LORD has made;
let us rejoice and be glad in it.
Psalm 118:24 NIV

The familiar words of Psalm 118:24 remind us of a profound yet simple truth: God created this day, and so we should rejoice in it and to be grateful for it. We give glory to our Creator when we treasure each day He gives us and use it to the fullest.

This day is a gift from God. How will you use it? Will you celebrate God's gifts and trust His promises? Will you share words of encouragement and hope with all who cross your path? Will you honor the Father by praising Him for His glorious handiwork?

Whatever this day holds for you, begin it and end it with God as your partner. Throughout the day, give thanks to the One who created it and filled it with wonderful opportunities just for you. God's love for you is infinite. Accept it joyously and be glad.

Men spend their lives in anticipation,
in determining to be vastly happy
at some period or other, when they have time.
But the present time has one advantage
over every other: it is ours.
Charles Caleb Colton

Relying on God

You are my God, and I will give you thanks;
you are my God, and I will exalt you.
Give thanks to the LORD, for he is good;
his love endures forever.
Psalm 118:28–29 NIV

The line from the children's song is reassuring and familiar: "Little ones to Him belong. We are weak but He is strong." That message applies to kids of all ages: we are all weak indeed, but we worship a mighty God who meets our needs and answers our prayers.

When we sincerely call upon our heavenly Father, He is a never-ending source of strength and courage. When we're weary, He gives us strength. When we see no hope, God reminds us of His promises. Whatever our circumstances, God will protect us and care for us . . . if we let Him.

Are you feeling weak or worried? If so, turn to God. Keep Him at the very center of your life and rely on Him. When you do, He will give you the direction and the strength you need.

The unfolding of our friendship with the Father
will be a never-ending revelation
stretching on into eternity.
Catherine Marshall

No Shortcuts

*Never be lazy, but work hard
and serve the Lord enthusiastically.*
Romans 12:11 NLT

The world often promises instant gratification: Get rich—quick. Lose weight—this week. Have whatever you want—right now. Yet life's experiences and God's Word teach us that the best things in life usually require heaping helpings of both time and work.

It has been said that there are no shortcuts to anyplace worth going. So it's important to remember that hard work is a proven way to get ahead; but more than that, it's also part of God's plan.

Today, do yourself this favor: don't look for shortcuts (because even if there are any, they're probably not worth taking), and don't expect easy solutions to life's big challenges (because big rewards usually require lots of effort). Promises of instant gratification abound, but the rewards of hard work are greater than any quick fix the world offers.

*I long to accomplish a great and noble task,
but it is my chief duty to accomplish small tasks
as if they were great and noble.*
Helen Keller

The Manual

He who despises the word will be destroyed,
but he who fears the commandment will be rewarded.
Proverbs 13:13 NKJV

The Bible contains God's promises, for which we should be eternally grateful. But that's not all. God's Word also contains thorough instructions which, if followed, lead to fulfillment, righteousness, and everlasting life. If we choose to ignore God's commandments, we forfeit those blessings. But if we obey God and revere Him, we will be blessed beyond measure.

Talking about God is easy; living by His Word is considerably harder. Yet unless we are willing to abide by God's laws, all of our righteous proclamations ring hollow. So how can we best proclaim our love for the Lord? By reading—and following—the manual He gave us. When we do, we'll see the wonderful fulfillment of God's promises in our lives.

Mary could not have dreamed all that would
result from her faithful obedience.
Likewise, you cannot possibly imagine all that God has in
store for you when you trust Him.
Henry Blackaby

Using Your Gifts to Serve

*Each of you should look not only to your own interests,
but also to the interests of others.*
Philippians 2:4 NIV

Jesus taught that the most esteemed men and women are not the leaders of society or the captains of industry. To the contrary, God's Word promises that the greatest among us will be those who choose to minister and to serve.

You may feel the temptation to build yourself up in the eyes of your neighbors. But resist that temptation. Instead, serve your neighbors quietly and without fanfare. Find a need and fill it . . . humbly. Lend a helping hand, even anonymously. Share a word of kindness.

Today, take the time to minister to those in need. Then, when you've done your best to serve your neighbors and to serve your God, you can rest comfortably knowing that in the eyes of God, you will be achieving greatness.

We have to serve God in His way, not in ours.
Saint Teresa of Avila

The Good Shepherd

The Lord is my shepherd. He gives me everything I need.
Psalm 23:1 NIrV

In the Twenty-third Psalm, David likened God to a watchful shepherd caring for His flock. The message is this: You are precious in the eyes of God. He watches over every step you make and every breath you take, so you need never be afraid.

But sometimes fear has a way of slipping into the minds and hearts of even the most faithful men and women. On occasion you will confront circumstances that trouble you, even shake you to the very core of your soul. When you are afraid, trust in God. When you're worried, turn your concerns over to Him. When you're anxious, be still and meditate on God's promises. When you do, you'll feel His quiet assurance.

Place your life in God's hands today. You can trust the Good Shepherd to guide you through your day, your life, and into eternity.

If a person fears God, he or she has no reason to fear anything else. On the other hand, if a person does not fear God, then fear becomes a way of life.
Beth Moore

About Anger

When you are angry, do not sin, and be sure to stop
being angry before the end of the day.
Do not give the devil a way to defeat you.
Ephesians 4:26–27 NCV

Sometimes anger is appropriate. Even Jesus became angry when He saw and confronted the money changers in the temple. On occasion, you, like Jesus, will confront evil; and when you do, you may respond vigorously and without reservation. But more often than not, your ire will be of the more mundane variety, in response to the various frustrations of everyday living.

In the course of your life, you will face countless opportunities to lose your temper over small, relatively insignificant events: a traffic jam, a spilled cup of coffee, an inconsiderate comment, a broken promise. When you're tempted to lose your temper over these sorts of irritants, take a step back. Turn away from anger, hatred, bitterness, and regret. Turn instead to God.

Anger is never without a reason,
but seldom a good one.
Ben Franklin

Beyond Bitterness

A man's wisdom gives him patience;
it is to his glory to overlook an offense.
Proverbs 19:11 NIV

Are you mired in the quicksand of bitterness or regret? If so, remember that the world holds few rewards for those who remain angrily focused on the past. Still, the act of forgiveness is difficult for even the most saintly men and women.

Being frail, fallible, imperfect human beings, most of us are quick to anger, quick to blame, slow to forgive, and even slower to forget. Yet we are instructed to forgive others, just as we have been forgiven by God.

Today, ask your Father in heaven to erase any bitterness from your heart. When you let go of your hurt and anger, you'll be making your corner of the world—and every corner of your heart—a kinder, gentler, happier place.

Let us not throw away any of our days
on useless resentment.
Samuel Johnson

The Gift of Cheerfulness

A miserable heart means a miserable life;
a cheerful heart fills the day with song.
Proverbs 15:15 MSG

Cheerfulness is a gift we give to others—and to ourselves. As we cheer other people up, we inevitably cheer ourselves up, too. But the opposite is also true: we cannot bring other people down without bringing ourselves down with them.

Are you a cheerful person most of the time? Do you go out of your way to make other people smile? You should—after all, sometimes it seems there's a worldwide shortage of folks who are willing to share a smile, a hug, a laugh, or a kind word.

Every family, every school, every workplace, every church, and every community can stand at least one more cheerful person. So don't delay—be cheerful today. The world needs your gift of cheerfulness . . . and so do you!

Cheerfulness strengthens the heart
and makes us try harder to have a good life,
thus God's servants must always be in good spirits.
Saint Philip Neri

At the End of the Rope

The LORD is a shelter for the oppressed, a refuge in times of trouble. Those who know your name trust in you, for you, O LORD, do not abandon those who search for you.
Psalm 9:9–10 NLT

Perhaps you've heard the saying "When you get to the end of your rope, tie a knot and hold on!" It's pithy, good advice, but here's something else to think about: when you get to the end of your rope, you don't have to hang on alone—because God is right there with you. So as you're trying hard to tie the best knot you can, do so with confidence. No matter where you are, no matter how desperate your circumstances, God never leaves you, not even for an instant. You belong to Him—you are His precious child and His one-of-a-kind creation.

The next time you find yourself at the end of your rope, take heart. You've got Company with a capital C. He will be your refuge and help.

Often God shuts a door in our face
so that He can open the door
through which He wants us to go.
Catherine Marshall

The God Who Never Leaves

No, I will not abandon you as orphans—I will come to you.
John 14:18 NLT

Doubts come in many shapes and sizes: doubts about God, doubts about the future, and doubts about our own abilities, for starters. But when doubts creep in, as they will from time to time, we need not despair. We need only turn to God.

When we turn to God sincerely and prayerfully, He is always available. He never leaves our side, not even for an instant. His love never waivers, His compassion never ceases, and His promises never fail.

Because the Creator is always with us, He can always calm the storms of life. When we earnestly seek Him—and when we strive to establish a deeper, more meaningful relationship with Him—God is prepared to soothe our hearts, to calm our fears, to answer our doubts, and to restore our confidence.

> *To wrestle with God does not mean*
> *that we have lost faith,*
> *but that we are fighting for it.*
> Sheila Walsh

Living in a Fearful World

I sought the LORD, and he answered me;
he delivered me from all my fears.
Psalm 34:4 NIV

We live in a fearful world, where bad news seems to travel at the speed of light, and good news at a snail's pace . . . if it gets communicated at all. These are troubled times, times when we have legitimate fears for the future of our families, our nation, and our world. But we have every reason to live courageously. After all, the ultimate battle has already been fought and won on that faraway cross at Calvary.

Perhaps your courage is being tested, and you feel barraged by the anxieties and fears that seem a pervasive part of twenty-first-century life. If so, take your concerns to God. Your heavenly Father is also your Protector and your Deliverer. Call upon Him in your hour of need, and be comforted. Whatever your challenge, whatever your trouble, God can handle it. When you call, He will answer.

When once we are assured that God is good,
then there can be nothing left to fear.
Hannah Whitall Smith

The Wisdom of Respect

The fear of the LORD is the beginning of wisdom,
and the knowledge of the Holy One is understanding.
Proverbs 9:10 NKJV

Do you have a healthy respect for God's power? If so, you are both wise and obedient. You also understand that genuine wisdom begins with a profound appreciation for God's limitless power.

The good news is this: when you develop a genuine, healthy fear of God's power, you'll soon discover that other fears—those nameless fears and worries that accompany the challenges of everyday life—begin to evaporate like the morning dew on a sunny summer's day.

So today, and every day hereafter, remind yourself of these truths: God is great; He is all-knowing; He is all-powerful; and He deserves your profound respect. And while you're at it, remind yourself that when you give Him the respect He deserves, you'll be both wise *and* courageous.

The remarkable thing about fearing God is that when you
fear God, you fear nothing else, whereas
if you do not fear God, you fear everything else.
Oswald Chambers

God's Forgiveness

You know the Lord is full of mercy and is kind.
James 5:11 NCV

God's capacity to forgive, like His love, is infinite. Despite our shortcomings, despite our sins, God offers immediate forgiveness and eternal life when we surrender and commit ourselves to Him.

Once we have received God's forgiveness, how then should we behave toward others? Should we remain embittered and resentful, or should we forgive them (just as God has forgiven us)? God's Word gives us the answer: we must show mercy and forgive others (Matthew 6:14–15; 18:21–22). When we do, we not only obey God's command, but we also free ourselves from a prison of our own making.

When it comes to forgiveness, God doesn't play favorites, and neither should you. Complete forgiveness is His way; make it your way, too.

The fact is, God no longer deals with us in judgment but in mercy. If people got what they deserved, this old planet would have ripped apart at the seams centuries ago. Praise God that because of His great love "we are not consumed, for his compassions never fail" (Lamentations 3:22).
Joni Eareckson Tada

March

Who Rules

You shall have no other gods before Me.
Exodus 20:3 NKJV

Who rules your heart? Is it God, or is it something else? Do you give God your first consideration, or is He nearer your last? Have you offered Him your heart, your soul, your talents, and your time, or have you given Him little more than a few hours each Sunday morning?

In the book of Exodus, God warns that we should place no gods before Him. Yet all too often we let Him fall to second, third, or fourth place as we unintentionally worship other things. When we find ourselves making possessions or interpersonal relationships a higher priority than loving our Father in heaven, it's time to seek His forgiveness and change our ways.

Does God rule your heart? Make certain that the honest answer to this question is a resounding yes. In the life of every child of God, the Father should come first. Make that a promise to Him—and to yourself—today.

The God who dwells in heaven
is willing to dwell also in the heart
of the humble believer.
Warren Wiersbe

A Life of Worship

God is sheer being itself–Spirit.
Those who worship him must do it out of their very being,
their spirits, their true selves, in adoration.
John 4:24 MSG

To truly know God, we must spend time with Him each day in worship and communion. Yet in a world filled with distractions, we can be sorely tempted to skimp on this practice.

Every life is based on some form of worship. The question is not whether we will worship but what we will worship. When we choose to worship God—and only God—every day of our lives, with no exception and with our very being, offering our spirits and our true selves to Him in adoration, that is true worship.

When you commit yourself to a life of worship, your heavenly Father will shower you with spiritual blessings that are beyond your best expectations.

When you use your life for God's glory,
everything you do can become an act of worship.
Rick Warren

Infinite Possibilities

*We know that all things work together for the good
of those who love God: those who are called
according to His purpose.*
Romans 8:28 HCSB

Ours is a God of infinite possibilities. But sometimes, because of our limited faith and limited understanding, we wrongly assume that God cannot or will not intervene in the affairs of mankind. But that's simply untrue. God's Word contains countless examples—and promises—that God does indeed work in people's lives . . . sometimes even doing the seemingly impossible.

Are you afraid to ask God to do big things in your life? Is your faith threadbare and worn? If so, it's time to abandon your doubts and reclaim your faith in God's promises.

Absolutely nothing is impossible for God. And since the Bible means what it says, you can be comforted in the knowledge that the Creator of the universe can do miraculous things in your own life and in the lives of your loved ones. So today, take God at His word, and expect the miraculous.

*The task ahead of us is never as great
as the Power behind us.*
Source unknown

God's Love and Protection

The LORD your God in your midst, The Mighty One,
will save; He will rejoice over you with gladness,
He will quiet you with His love,
He will rejoice over you with singing.
Zephaniah 3:17 NKJV

The arms of God encircle us and comfort us in times of adversity. In times of hardship He restores our strength; in times of sorrow He dries our tears. When we are troubled or weak or embittered, God is as near as our next breath.

The Mighty One has promised to watch over us and keep us, and He always keeps His promises. In a world filled with dangers and temptations, God is the ultimate armor. In a world filled with misleading messages, God's Word is the ultimate truth. In a world filled with more frustrations than we can count, God offers the ultimate peace.

Will you accept God's love and protection and wear His armor against the dangers of our world? When you do, you can live courageously, trusting in God's unfailing love for you.

God will never let you sink under
your circumstances. He always provides
a safety net and His love always encircles.
Barbara Johnson

When Hope Slips Away

Hope deferred makes the heart sick.
Proverbs 13:12 NKJV

Have you ever felt your hopes for the future slipping away? If so, perhaps you've temporarily lost sight of the hope that followers of God must place in the promises of God. If you're feeling discouraged, worried, or worse, remember the words of Psalm 31:24 (NKJV): "Be of good courage, and He shall strengthen your heart."

Because of God's promises, we can have hope for the future—no matter how desperate our circumstances may seem. After all, God has promised to keep us as His own for all eternity if we will place our hope and trust in Him.

Yes, we will face disappointments and failures in life; but these are only temporary defeats. This world can be a place of trials and tribulations, yet when our hope is in God, we are secure. God promises peace, joy, and eternal life. Accept His gifts today, and never let your hope slip away.

Teach us to set our hopes on heaven,
to hold firmly to the promise of eternal life,
so that we can withstand the struggles
and storms of this world.
Max Lucado

Kindness in Action

*Yes indeed, it is good when you obey the royal law
as found in the Scriptures:
"Love your neighbor as yourself."*
James 2:8 NLT

In the busyness and confusion of daily life, it's easy to lose focus, and it's easy to become frustrated. But God's Word tells us we should show concern for our neighbors, and that includes when we're tired, busy, frustrated . . . or all of the above.

Today, as you consider all the wonderful things God has done for you, honor Him by being kind to one of His children. Honor Him by slowing down long enough to say an extra word of encouragement to someone who needs it. Honor Him by picking up the phone and calling a distant friend, if for no reason other than to say, "I'm thinking of you." When you honor God by following His command to love others, you'll find that, as promised, it's a good thing.

*No one is useless in the world who lightens
the burden of it to anyone else.*
Charles Dickens

Living Life Fully

Show me, O LORD, my life's end and the number of
my days; let me know how fleeting is my life.
You have made my days a mere handbreadth;
the span of my years is as nothing before you.
Each man's life is but a breath.
Psalm 39:4–5 NIV

Because our time here on earth is brief, every day is precious. Each day is a nonrenewable resource—once it's gone, it's gone forever. If we are thoughtful, we'll recognize the brevity of life; and if we're thankful, we'll become fully engaged in the opportunities and responsibilities around us.

Do you view this day as a one-of-a-kind opportunity to do your work, to count your blessings, to develop your talents, and to celebrate your life? Have you formed the habit of tackling first things first? And do you thank your Creator many times each day for gifts He has given you in that day? Today, act in such a way that you can answer these questions with a resounding yes. After all, today is already here, but it will soon be gone. Be sure you live it to the fullest.

The proper function of mankind is to live,
not to exist.
Jack London

Making Peace with the Past

*Do not remember the past events, pay no attention
to things of old. Look, I am about to do something new;
even now it is coming. Do you not see it? Indeed,
I will make a way in the wilderness, rivers in the desert.*
Isaiah 43:17–19 HCSB

Have you made peace with your past? If so, congratulations. If not, today is a golden opportunity to change your thoughts and, by extension, your life. How can you change? By accepting what has been and by trusting God for what will be.

As frail humans, we can be slow to forget ___day's disappointments. If that sounds like you, ___ not alone. But if you sincerely desire to focus ___opes and energies on the future, then you must ___ays to accept the past, no matter how difficult ___seem to do so.

___you have not yet made peace with your past, ___s the day to declare an end to all hostilities. ___ur past to the God of all time, and lay it at His ___en turn your thoughts to wondrous promises ___ and to the glorious future He has in store

There is no road back to yesterday.
Oswald Chambers

Pleasing the Crowd

*My dear friends, don't let public opinion influence
how you live out our glorious, Christ-originated faith.*
James 2:1 MSG

As a member of this highly competitive twenty-first-century world, you know that the demands and expectations of everyday living can seem burdensome, even overwhelming at times. Keeping up with the Joneses can become a full-time job if you let it. But a better strategy is to stop trying to please the neighbors and to concentrate, instead, on pleasing God.

Perhaps you have set your goals high; if so, congratulations! You're willing to dream big dreams, and that's a good thing. But as you consider your life's path and purpose, don't allow your quest for excellence to interfere with the spiritual journey that God has planned for you. All other concerns—including pleasing the crowd—are of little importance compared with your faith.

*If a million people believe a foolish thing,
it is still a foolish thing.*
Anatole France

The Antidote to Fear

When I am afraid, I will trust in You.
Psalm 56:3 HCSB

Considered by some to be the most popular cowgirl of her time, Dale Evans starred with cowboy husband Roy Rogers and she wrote their theme song, "Happy Trails." Dale once said, "I have found the perfect antidote for fear. Whenever it sticks up its ugly face, I clobber it with prayer."

In the Bible, the psalmist said, "In my distress I prayed to the LORD, and the LORD answered me and set me free" (118:5 NLT). And God will do the same for you. So if you've been beset by the fears that grip us all from time to time, pray for courage . . . and keep praying. When you do, much like Dale Evans, you'll enjoy plenty of clear skies and lots of happy trails.

God makes prayer as easy as possible for us.
He's completely approachable and available,
and He'll never mock or upbraid us
for bringing our needs before Him.
Shirley Dobson

Pride in Abundance

When pride comes, disgrace follows,
but with humility comes wisdom.
Proverbs 11:2 HCSB

Sometimes we are tested more in times of plenty than we are in times of privation. When we experience life's difficult days, we may be quick to turn our thoughts and hearts to God, looking for help. But in times of plenty, when the sun is shining and our minds are at ease, we may be tempted to think our good fortune is of our own making. Nothing could be further from the truth. God plays a hand in every aspect of everyday life, and for the blessings we receive, we must offer thanks and praise to Him.

Have you been blessed by God? Are you enjoying the abundance He has provided? If so, praise Him for His gifts. Praise Him faithfully and humbly. And don't, for a single moment, allow a prideful heart to separate you from the blessings of your loving, heavenly Father.

God gives grace to the humble,
not to the prideful. If we assume self-advancing attitudes,
we've missed His gift of favor.
Franklin Graham

Renewed Strength

Be strengthened by the Lord and by His vast strength.
Ephesians 6:10 HCSB

God promises that when we genuinely lift our hearts and prayers to Him, He will renew our strength.

Are you weary and worn? Go to God in prayer. Are you weak or worried? Delve deeply into God's Word; bask in His promises and sense His presence in the quiet moments of the day. Are you exhausted, either physically, emotionally, or spiritually? Call upon encouraging friends to support you, but most importantly, call upon God to renew your strength and your courage. Your Creator is always available, and He will not let you down. To the contrary, He will lift you up when you ask Him to do so. Go to Him today and receive the promised blessing of renewed strength.

Jesus is calling the weary to rest,
Calling today, calling today,
Bring Him your burden and you shall be blest;
He will not turn you away.
Fanny Crosby

Simplicity

*Whoever becomes simple and elemental again,
like this child, will rank high in God's kingdom.*
Matthew 18:4 MSG

We live in a world where simplicity seems in short supply. Think for a moment about the complexity of your everyday life and compare it to the lives of your ancestors. Certainly, you are the beneficiary of many technological innovations, but those innovations can come with a price: in all likelihood, your world is highly complex.

Unless you take firm control of your time and your life, you risk being overwhelmed by the ever-growing tidal wave of complexity that can, unchecked, threaten your happiness. But your heavenly Father knows the joy of living simply, and so can you. So do yourself a favor: keep your life as simple as possible. Simplicity is genius. By simplifying your life, you'll be amazed at how much you'll actually improve it.

*If you desire many things,
many things will seem but a few.*
Ben Franklin

Rebels Beware

*Whoever is stubborn after being corrected many times
will suddenly be hurt beyond cure.*
Proverbs 29:1 NCV

Since the days of Adam and Eve, human beings have been strong-willed and rebellious. Our rebellion stems, in large part, from an intense desire to do things our way instead of God's way. But when we choose to step off God's path for our lives, we do ourselves a profound injustice . . . and we will suffer because of our stubbornness.

God's Word instructs us to be humble, not prideful; obedient, not rebellious. God wants us to do things His way, but for good reason: when we do, we'll reap a bountiful harvest of blessings—more blessings than we can count.

God has created a world in which we reap what we sow. May we sow seeds of obedience . . . and reap God's blessings.

*A man's greatest enemies are
his own apathy and stubbornness.*
Frank Tyger

Time to Maturity

*Don't look for shortcuts to God. The market is flooded
with surefire, easygoing formulas for a successful life that
can be practiced in your spare time. Don't fall for that
stuff, even though crowds of people do. The way to life—
to God!—is vigorous and requires total attention.*
Matthew 7:13–14 MSG

Spiritual maturity takes time. We simply cannot
gain the perspective and insight we need by reading
a book or by listening to a sermon or by attending a
weekend seminar. Of course, we all experience those
"aha! moments" when we gain a rush of insight. But
even then, we don't become instantly mature. The real
core of wisdom comes not just from understanding
life's important principles but also from living in
accordance with those principles for years.

So if you're not quite as mature as you'd like to
be, don't be discouraged. There are no instantaneous
saints. But there are plenty of people (like you) who
are slowly becoming more mature, and more saintly,
day by day.

*I've never met anyone who became instantly mature.
It's a painstaking process that God takes us through,
and it includes such things as waiting, failing, losing, and
being misunderstood—each calling
for extra doses of perseverance.*
Charles Swindoll

Beyond Blame

His disciples asked, "Rabbi, who sinned: this man or his
parents, causing him to be born blind?" Jesus said,
"You're asking the wrong question. You're looking for
someone to blame. There is no such cause-effect here.
Look instead for what God can do."
John 9:1–3 MSG

To blame others for our problems is the height of futility. Yet blaming others is so easy to do, and improving ourselves is much harder. So instead of solving problems, we're often tempted to fret over the perceived unfairness of life while doing little else.

Are you looking for an ironclad formula for problem solving that will leave you happier, healthier, and wiser? Then don't play the blame game. It's a game in which all the participants lose.

When Jesus's followers looked for someone to blame, the Master warned them to refrain from such shortsightedness. And we should do likewise. Then, when we've made peace with the past, we can focus upon the future . . . and the wonderful things God can do.

The entirety of one's adult life is a series of personal
choices, decisions. If they [people] can accept this totally,
then they become free people. To the extent that they do
not accept this, they will forever feel themselves victims.
M. Scott Peck

A Proper Mind-set

Set your minds on what is above,
not on what is on the earth.
Colossians 3:2 HCSB

What have you set your mind on today? What attitude have you chosen? Are you fearful, angry, bored, or worried? Are you more concerned about pleasing your friends than about pleasing your God? Are you confused, bitter, or pessimistic? If so, perhaps it's time to redirect your attention to things above—on the things of God.

God created you in His own image, and He wants you to experience joy and abundance. But God will never demand that you be joyful; you must choose this spiritual treasure for yourself. So today, and every day hereafter, choose to focus on God and His many blessings. When you do, you'll find it easy to celebrate this life He has given you. You'll think optimistically about your life and your future.

Give thanks to the One who has given you everything, and trust in your heart that He wants to give you much, much more.

The greater part of our happiness or misery depends on our
dispositions, and not our circumstances.
Martha Washington

Keeping Up Appearances

If you decide for God, living a life of God-worship,
it follows that you don't fuss about what's on the table
at mealtimes or whether the clothes in your closet are in
fashion. There is far more to your life than the food you
put in your stomach, more to your outer appearance
than the clothes you hang on your body.
Matthew 6:25 MSG

Are you worried about keeping up appearances? Do you spend too much time, energy, or money on things that are intended to make you look good? If so, you're certainly not alone. Ours is a society that seems obsessed with appearances. We're told that we can't be too thin or too rich. But in truth, the important things in life have little to do with food, fashion, fame, or fortune.

Today, spend less time trying to please the world and more time tring to please God and loving your family and friends. It takes too much energy to keep up appearances. And God promises us a life much better than a mere fashion show when we decide to live for Him.

What I must do is all that concerns me,
not what people think.
Ralph Waldo Emerson

Being Part of God's Church

The church, you see, is not peripheral to the world;
the world is peripheral to the church.
The church is Christ's body, in which he speaks and acts,
by which he fills everything with his presence.
Ephesians 1:23 MSG

One way to enjoy more of God's promised blessings is to become involved in God's church.

Are you an active, contributing, member of your local fellowship? The answer to this simple question will have a profound impact on the quality of your spiritual journey.

So if you're not currently engaged in a local church, do yourself a favor: find a church you're comfortable with and join it. And once you've joined, don't just attend services out of habit. Go to church out of a sincere desire to know and worship God. When you do, you'll be blessed by the men and women who attend your fellowship, and you'll be blessed by your Creator—because His church is filled with His presence.

Don't ever come to church without coming
as though it were the first time, as though
it could be the best time, and as though
it might be the last time.
Vance Havner

When People Misbehave

Sensible people control their temper;
they earn respect by overlooking wrongs.
Proverbs 19:11 NLT

Sometimes people can be discourteous or even cruel. They can be unfair, unkind, and unappreciative. Sometimes they get angry and frustrated. So what's a person to do when others behave in such ways? God's answer is straightforward: forgive. In Luke 6:37, Jesus instructs, "Do not judge, and you will not be judged. Do not condemn, and you will not be condemned. Forgive, and you will be forgiven" (HCSB).

Today and every day, determine to be quick to forgive others for their shortcomings. And when the people around you misbehave (as they will from time to time), remember that we all (yourself included) have moments when we're not at our best. Just forgive the offender as quickly as you can, and try to move on . . . as quickly as you can.

Our forgiveness toward others should flow
from a realization and appreciation
of God's forgiveness toward us.
Franklin Graham

Taking Care of Your Dreams

*Each generation should set its hope anew on God,
not forgetting his glorious miracles
and obeying his commands.*
Psalm 78:7 NLT

Having spent much of his boyhood on a Missouri farm, Walt Disney had plenty of time to dream, filling his head with visions of delightful characters that would one day come to life on the movie and television screen. In fact, Disney himself was the first voice of his most notable creation: Mickey Mouse. And Walt's legacy continues today, still going . . . and still growing.

Disney once said, "All our dreams can come true if we only have the courage to pursue them." He built a legacy on that philosophy.

All of us should carefully nurture our hopes and dreams. Because as Walt Disney demonstrated, when we dare to dream big, big dreams have a way of coming true.

*Dream lofty dreams, and as you dream,
so shall you become.*
John Ruskin

Faith for the Future

We walk by faith, not by sight.
2 Corinthians 5:7 NKJV

The first element of a successful life is faith: faith in God and faith in His promises. If we place our lives in God's hands, our faith will be rewarded in ways that we—as human beings with clouded vision and limited understanding—can scarcely comprehend. But if we rely only on our own resources, or if we seek earthly success outside the boundaries of God's guidelines, we'll reap a bitter harvest.

Do you desire the abundant life that God has promised? Then trust Him today and every day that you live. Trust Him with every aspect of your life. And trust His promises. Then, when you have placed your future in the hands of the Giver of all good things, rest assured that your future is secure—not only for today but for all eternity.

Worry and anxiety are sand in the machinery of life; faith is the oil.
E. Stanley Jones

Talking to Yourself

I said to myself,
"Relax and rest. GOD has showered you with blessings."
Psalm 116:7 MSG

Do you spend much time talking to yourself? If so, don't worry—you're not crazy. To the contrary, you may be very wise indeed, especially if you've learned how to talk to yourself properly.

Do you remind yourself each day of God's blessings? Do you advise the person in the mirror to be thankful, thoughtful, patient, and kind? And do you encourage yourself to trust God's Word and to follow His path? If you can answer these questions positively, you are both wise and blessed.

In Psalm 116, the psalmist reminded himself of God's blessings. You should, too. So today, talk to yourself about the Father's love, about His gifts, and about His teachings. Focus on the Father and enjoy a peace like no other.

The things we think are the things that feed
our souls. If we think on pure and lovely things,
we shall grow pure and lovely like them;
and the converse is equally true.
Hannah Whitall Smith

Giving Freely

*Give, and you will receive. Your gift will return
to you in full—pressed down, shaken together to make room
for more, running over, and poured into your lap.
The amount you give will determine
the amount you get back.*
Luke 6:38 NLT

The Bible makes an important promise: if you give, you will receive. If you give generously of your time, your possessions, your talents, and your love, you will be blessed in return by your Creator.

Your life is a tapestry of decisions. Each day you face choices concerning the things (material and nonmaterial) you should keep for yourself and the things you should give away. What will you decide? When in doubt, why not err on the side of generosity?

Be quick to share a smile, an encouraging word, a pat on the back, a helping hand, or a heartfelt hug. Be more concerned with giving than getting. Weave the habit of generosity into the fabric of your day. When you do, everybody wins . . . and you'll be the biggest winner of all.

*There is no happiness in having, or in getting,
but only in giving.*
Henry Drummond

God's Wondrous Handiwork

The heavens declare the glory of God,
and the sky proclaims the work of His hands.
Psalm 19:1 HCSB

When we pause to examine God's wondrous handiwork, one thing becomes clear: God is, indeed, a miracle worker. Throughout history He has intervened in the course of human events in ways which can't be explained away by science or human rationale.

God's miracles are not limited to special occasions, nor are they witnessed only by a select few. God is crafting His wonders all around us: the miracle of a newborn baby; the miracle of a world renewing itself with every sunrise; the miracle of lives transformed by God's love and by His grace. Each day God's miraculous handiwork is evident for all to see—and available for all to experience.

The psalmist reminds us that the heavens are a declaration of God's glory. May we never cease to praise the Creator for a universe that stands as an awesome testimony to His presence, to His power, and to His love.

All of creation is a song of praise to God.
Hildegard of Bingen

God's Love, God's Power

Our Lord is great, vast in power;
His understanding is infinite.
Psalm 147:5 HCSB

God's power is not hampered by boundaries or limitations—and neither is His love. The love that flows from the heart of God is infinite, and today offers us the opportunity to celebrate that love.

Have you genuinely allowed God to reign over every part of your heart, or have you attempted to confine Him to a spiritual compartment? How you answer that question will determine the quality and direction not just of your spiritual life but of your whole life.

God stands at the door of your heart and waits. Welcome Him in today, and allow Him to rule. When you do, you'll enjoy the peace, the protection, and the abundance that only God can give—and that He promises to those who ask.

God will never let you be shaken or moved
from your place near His heart.
Joni Eareckson Tada

Trusting God's Timing

*Humble yourselves under the mighty hand of God,
that He may exalt you in due time.*
1 Peter 5:6 NKJV

If you sincerely desire to be a person of faith, one important part of that is to trust God's timing. Certainly it's easy not to trust His timing. It's tempting to take things into our own hands. Because we are fallible human beings, we're impatient for things to happen. But sometimes we have to wait. Sometimes we have to remind ourselves that God knows better.

Our heavenly Father has created a world that turns according to His timetable, not ours . . . thank goodness! We mortals might make a terrible mess of things.

God's plan does not always unfold in the way we would like or at the time of our choosing. But our task—as people who trust in a benevolent, all-knowing Father—is to wait patiently for God to reveal Himself. And reveal Himself He will. But until God's perfect plan is made known, we must walk in faith and never lose hope. He will work things out in due time—His time.

*God is in no hurry. Compared to the works of mankind,
He is extremely deliberate.
God is not a slave to the human clock.*
Charles Swindoll

Imitating Christ

*I have given you an example that you also should do
just as I have done for you.*
John 13:15 HCSB

Life is a series of choices. Each day we make countless decisions that can bring us closer to God . . . or pull us away from Him. When we live according to God's commandments, we'll reap bountiful rewards: spiritual abundance, hope, and peace, for starters.

Do you seek to walk in the footsteps of Jesus, or will you choose another path? If you sincerely desire God's peace and His blessings, then you must strive to imitate God's Son.

Thomas Brooks once said, "Christ is the sun, and all the watches of our lives should be set by the dial of his motion." Christ, indeed, is the ultimate example for mankind. May we strive to walk in His footsteps as we share His love and His message with a world that needs both.

*When we look into the mirror,
may we see more and more of Him.*
Marilyn Meberg

Today with God

Seek the LORD, and ye shall live.
Amos 5:6 KJV

Life is a glorious gift from God. Are you treating it that way? This day, like every other, is filled to the brim with opportunities, challenges, and choices. But no choice that you make is more important than the choice you make concerning God. You can choose to place Him at the center of your life, or you can relegate Him to the sidelines.

We don't always intentionally neglect God; sometimes we simply allow ourselves to become preoccupied with the business of living. And then, without our even realizing it, we gradually drift away from the One we need most. But God never drifts away from us. He remains always present, always steadfast, always loving.

As you begin this day, place God first in your thoughts, in your prayers, on your lips, and in your heart. Begin today with God. You'll find no better guide and companion in the business of living.

There is nothing more important in any life
than the constantly enjoyed presence of the Lord.
There is nothing more vital, for without it we shall make
mistakes, and without it we shall be defeated.
Alan Redpath

On Mistakes and Lessons

I used to wander off until you disciplined me;
but now I closely follow your word.
Psalm 119:67 NLT

Have you experienced a setback recently? If so, have you looked for the lesson God may be trying to teach you through that experience? Instead of complaining about life's sad state of affairs, take the opportunity to learn what needs to be learned, change what needs to be changed . . . so you're equipped to move on to the next set of challenges. View failure as an opportunity to reassess God's will for your life. And while you're at it, learn to see life's inevitable disappointments as occasions to learn more—more about yourself, more about your circumstances, and more about your world.

Life can be difficult at times, and everybody (including you) makes mistakes. The key is to make them only once. And how can you do that? By learning the lessons of tough times sooner rather than later; and by closely following God's Word from this moment forward.

Success is going from failure to failure
without loss of enthusiasm.
Winston Churchill

Making God's Perspective Your Perspective

LORD, You light my lamp;
my God illuminates my darkness.
Psalm 18:28 HCSB

Sometimes, amid the demands of daily living, life can feel out of balance. The pressures we face may seem overwhelming. What's needed is a fresh perspective, a restored sense of balance . . . and God.

If a temporary loss of perspective has left you worried, exhausted, or both, it's time to readjust your thought patterns. Negative thoughts are habit-forming; fortunately, so are positive ones. With practice, you can form the habit of focusing on God's priorities and dwelling on possibilities rather than problems. When you do, you'll soon discover that you spend less time fretting about your challenges and more time praising God for His gifts.

When you make God's priorities your priorities, He will direct your steps and calm your fears. So today and every day, pray for a sense of balance . . . and a glimpse of things from God's perspective.

Earthly fears are no fears at all.
Answer the big question of eternity,
and the little questions of life fall into perspective.
Max Lucado

April

More Praise, More Hope

I will always have hope; I will praise you more and more.
Psalm 71:14 NIV

Praise and hope are traveling companions: the more we praise God, the more confident we'll become in His ability to revolutionize our days and our lives.

Have you formed the habit of praising God many times each day for His blessings? Do you thank Him often for who He is and what He has done for you? Once you form the habit of praising your heavenly Father many times throughout the day, you'll find your spirits lifted right along with your hopes.

Today, as the sun peeks over the horizon, God will once again shower you with more gifts than you can count. Thank Him, trust Him, follow Him . . . and match the size of your hopes to the size of God's promises.

> *Praising God reduces your cares,*
> *levels your anxieties,*
> *and multiplies your blessings.*
> Suzanne Dale Ezell

Our Rock and Help

Our help is in the name of the LORD,
the Maker of heaven and earth.
Psalm 124:8 HCSB

Our search to discover God's plan for our lives is not a destination to be reached; it is a path to be traveled, a journey that unfolds day by day. And that's exactly how we should seek direction from our Creator: one step at a time, one day at a time . . . each day followed by the next, without exception.

Life is a series of changes and adjustments: how far we go depends upon how well we adjust. Sometimes the adjustments are easy; sometimes they're not. But we can find comfort in the knowledge that our heavenly Father is the Rock that cannot be shaken.

Have you endured changes that left your head spinning and your heart aching? If so, seek help from the Maker of heaven and earth. The same God who created the universe will take your hand and walk with you if you ask Him . . . so ask Him! Then serve Him with willing hands and a trusting heart.

The Rock of Ages is the great sheltering encirclement.
Oswald Chambers

Walking with God

By this we know that we have come to know Him,
if we keep His commandments.
1 John 2:3 NASB

How do others know that we are walking with God? By our words and by our actions. And when it comes to proclaiming our faith, the actions we take are far more important than the proclamations we make.

Is your conduct a worthy example for others? Is your behavior a testimony to the spiritual abundance that is available to those who allow God to reign over their hearts? If so, congratulations! If you're like most of us, though, you're aware of some important aspect of your life that could stand improvement.

Today is the perfect day to step out in faith and determine to be a living, breathing example of the wonderful changes God can make in the lives of those who choose to walk with Him. What are you waiting for?

It is God to whom and with whom we travel;
while He is the End of our journey,
He is also at every stopping place.
Elisabeth Elliot

Wise Words

From a wise mind comes wise speech;
the words of the wise are persuasive.
Proverbs 16:23 NLT

Think, pause . . . *then* speak: how wise is the person who can communicate in this way. But all too often, in the rush to be heard, we speak first and think next . . . with unfortunate results.

God's Word teaches us that reckless words pierce like a sword, but the tongue of the wise brings healing (Proverbs 12:18).

If we want to be a source of encouragement to friends and family, then we must measure our words carefully. So today, make it a point to encourage all who cross your path. Measure your words carefully. Speak wisely, not impulsively. Use words of kindness and praise, not words of anger or derision. Remember that your words have power to heal others or to injure them, to lift others up or to drag them down. When you use wise words, you'll bring healing and comfort to a world that needs both.

God gave us two ears and one mouth,
so we ought to listen twice as much as we speak.
Irish proverb

Beyond Negativity

A word out of your mouth may seem of no account,
but it can accomplish nearly anything—or destroy it!
James 3:5 MSG

From experience, we know that it's easier to criticize than to correct, that it's easier to find faults than solutions, and that excessive criticism is usually destructive, not productive. Yet the urge to criticize others remains a powerful one for most of us. Since criticism is an expression of negative thinking, we must find a way to break the twin habits of negative thinking and critical speech.

As you examine the quality of your own comments, can you honestly say you're a cheerleader, not a critic? If so, keep up the good words. But if you occasionally fall into negativity, and if you pass that negativity along to others, perhaps it's time for a mental housecleaning. Start by redirecting your thoughts to all the blessings God has given you. When our hearts are filled with God's love, that's what will flow out of our lips as well.

After one hour in heaven,
we shall be ashamed that we ever grumbled.
Vance Havner

Where to Take Your Concerns

*Do not worry about anything,
but pray and ask God for everything you need,
always giving thanks.*
Philippians 4:6 NCV

In the game of life, you win some and you lose some. Living is risky business; ours is an uncertain world, a world in which trouble may come calling at any moment. No wonder you may find yourself feeling a little panicky at times.

Do you sometimes spend more time worrying about a problem than you spend solving it? If so, here's a strategy for dealing with your worries: take them to God. Take your troubles to Him; take your fears to Him; take your doubts to Him; take your weaknesses to Him; take your sorrows to Him . . . and leave them all there. Your heavenly Father has promised to take care of you; so ask God for what you need, and remember to give Him thanks for all He's provided (and will provide). Then you'll have absolutely no need to worry . . . not now, not ever.

*Worry is interest paid on trouble
before it comes due.*
William Ralph Inge

Working for Wisdom

Wisdom is a tree of life to those who embrace her;
happy are those who hold her tightly.
Proverbs 3:18 NLT

All of us would like to be wise, but not all of us are willing to do the work that is required to become wise. Wisdom is not like a mushroom; it doesn't spring up overnight. It's more like an oak tree that starts as a tiny acorn, grows into a sapling, and eventually reaches up to the sky, tall and strong.

To become wise, we must do the work of seeking God and living according to His Word. To become wise, we must pursue wisdom. We must not only learn the lessons of life; we must live by them.

Do you desire wisdom for yourself and for your family? Then keep learning from the Master—and keep motivating your family members to do likewise. Consult the ultimate source of wisdom, the Bible. When you study God's Word and live according to His commandments, you'll already be showing encouraging signs of wisdom . . . and you'll be a blessing to your family and to the world.

Our first step toward gaining God's wisdom
is to know what we do not know; that is,
to be aware of our shortcomings.
Dianna Booher

Working Hard

We want each of you to go on with the same hard work
all your lives so you will surely get what you hope for. . . .
Be like those who through faith and patience will receive
what God has promised.
Hebrews 6:11–12 NCV

Does God intend for us to work diligently, or does He endorse mediocrity? The answer should be obvious. God has created a world in which hard work is rewarded and sloppy work is not. Yet sometimes we may seek ease over excellence, or we may be tempted to take shortcuts. But God calls us to walk the straight and narrow path of hard work, faith, and patience.

Today, heed God's Word by doing good work. Wherever you find yourself, do your work well, and do it with all your heart. When you do, you may win the recognition of your peers or earn some earthly reward. But more important, God will bless your efforts and use you in ways that only He can orchestrate. So do your work with focus and dedication, because the reward God promises to the faithful is worth the effort.

Think enthusiastically about everything,
especially your work.
Norman Vincent Peale

Obedience and Peace

Those who love Your law have great peace,
and nothing causes them to stumble.
Psalm 119:165 NASB

Ours is a noisy, troubled world, a world in which peace can seem a scarce commodity—but it need not be so. The Bible promises that peace can be ours when we trust God's promises and obey His commandments. But the Bible also issues a warning: if we pay scant attention to God's Word, or if we rebel against His teachings altogether, we may forfeit countless blessings that might otherwise have been ours.

Would you like to enjoy the genuine, lasting peace that only God can provide? Then learn to love His Word by studying it and living by it. When you honor God with your actions, you'll soon discover that obedience is the path to peace. It always has been, and it always will be.

You cannot know and do the will of God
without paying the price of adjustment
and obedience.
Henry Blackaby

A Happy Heart

For the happy heart, life is a continual feast.
Proverbs 15:15 NLT

Happiness depends less on our circumstances than on our attitudes. When we turn our hearts and thoughts to God, rejoice in His gifts, and give thanks for His glorious creation, we will experience the joy that God intends for all of His children. But when we dwell on the negative aspects of life, we often bring needless pain to our friends, to our families, and to ourselves.

Do you sincerely want to be a happy person? Then set your mind and your heart on God's love and His grace. Seek a genuine, intimate, life-altering relationship with your Creator by reading His Word, talking to Him, and trusting His promises. Determine to count your blessings instead of your hardships. Then you'll know the joy, the peace, and the spiritual abundance that the Shepherd offers His sheep.

I became aware of one very important concept
I had missed before:
my attitude—not my circumstances—
was what was making me unhappy.
Vonette Bright

Enduring Hard Times

*God blesses those who patiently endure testing
and temptation. Afterward they will receive the crown
of life that God has promised to those who love him.*
James 1:12 NLT

As life unfolds, all of us suffer in some way. These occasional visits from Old Man Trouble are simply a fact of life, and none of us are exempt. When tough times arrive, we may be forced to rearrange our plans and our priorities. But even on our darkest days, we must remember that God's love remains constant. And we must never forget that God intends for us to use our setbacks as stepping-stones on the path to better lives.

When faced with tough times, we have a choice: we can begin the difficult work of tackling our troubles, going to God for help and healing; or we can choose defeat and surrender. If we choose the latter, even the smallest problems have a way of growing into king-size catastrophes. But when we patiently endure and have faith, God will not only help us today; He will reward us with a crown of life for eternity.

*If we make our troubles an opportunity to learn more of
God's love and His power to aid and bless
then they will teach us to have a firmer
confidence in His Providence.*
Billy Graham

Just Ask

You do not have because you do not ask.
James 4:2 HCSB

Sometimes, amid the demands and the frustrations of everyday life, we forget to slow down long enough to talk with—and listen to—God. Instead of turning our thoughts and prayers to Him, we rely on our own resources. Instead of praying for strength and courage, we try to manufacture it within ourselves. Instead of asking God for guidance, we depend on our own limited wisdom. The results of such decisions are unfortunate at best; at worst, they can be tragic.

Are you in need? Ask God to sustain you. Are you troubled? Take your worries to Him in prayer. Are you weary? Seek God's strength. In all things great and small, seek God's wisdom and His grace. He hears your prayers, and He will answer. All you must do is ask.

God will help us become the people
we are meant to be,
if only we will ask Him.
Hannah Whitall Smith

The Value of Good Advice

*Know-it-alls don't like being told what to do;
they avoid the company of wise men and women.*
Proverbs 15:12 MSG

It's a truism: advice is cheap. And sometimes advice is worth exactly what we pay for it: little or nothing. That's why it's so important to find friends and mentors whose advice you can trust. And then, once you've received their advice (and considered it in light of God's Word), be wise enough to take it.

Not everyone possesses the insight or the wisdom to provide you with sound, godly counsel. Are you walking with the wise? Are you spending time with people you trust and admire? Are you learning how to live from people who know how to live?

If you're wise, you will surround yourself with wise people, and you'll listen carefully to their words. If you desire to walk with God, you'll keep company with others who walk with Him, too.

*It takes a wise person to give good advice,
but an even wiser person to take it.*
Marie T. Freeman

When It's Hard to Be Cheerful

Be cheerful. Keep things in good repair.
Keep your spirits up. Think in harmony.
Be agreeable. Do all that, and the God of love
and peace will be with you for sure.
2 Corinthians 13:11 MSG

On some days it's hard to be cheerful. When the demands of the world around us increase and our energy flags, we feel less like cheering up and more like tearing up. But even in our darkest hours, we can turn to God, and He will give us comfort.

How can we experience the joyful abundance that God has promised? By giving Him what is rightfully His: our hearts, our minds . . . in short, our faithfulness. When we earnestly commit ourselves to God, when we place Him at the center of our lives, He will transform us—not just for today but for all eternity. Then we, as God's children, can share the Father's joy and His message with others finding it hard to be cheerful.

A cloudy day is no match for a sunny disposition.
William Arthur Ward

Threatened by the Storms of Life

He said to them, "Why are you fearful, you of little faith?"
Then He got up and rebuked the winds and the sea.
And there was a great calm.
Matthew 8:26 HCSB

A storm rose quickly on the Sea of Galilee, and the disciples were afraid. Although they had seen Jesus perform many miracles, the disciples feared for their lives; so they turned to their Master, and He calmed the waters and the wind.

Sometimes we, like the disciples, feel threatened by the storms of life. Thankfully, when we are fearful, we, too, can turn to Christ for courage and for comfort.

The next time you're afraid, remember that the One who calmed the wind and waves is also able to calm your heart and mind. He will save you if you trust in Him. Then, rather than feel threatened by the storms of life, we can face them courageously . . . and come through them safely.

You gain strength, courage and confidence
every time you look fear in the face.
Eleanor Roosevelt

Beyond Doubt

If any of you lacks wisdom, he should ask God,
who gives to all generously and without criticizing,
and it will be given to him. But let him ask in faith
without doubting. For the doubter is like the surging sea,
driven and tossed by the wind.
James 1:5–6 HCSB

If you've never had any doubts about your faith, then you can stop reading this page and skip to the next. But if you've ever been plagued by doubts about your faith or your God, keep reading.

Even some of the most faithful are beset by bouts of discouragement and doubt. But even when we feel far removed from God, God is never far removed from us. He is always with us, willing to give us wisdom and help, willing to replace our doubts with comfort and assurance.

When you take your doubts to God and let Him speak assurance to your heart, you'll find you can step beyond those doubts to a firmer foundation of faith.

The strengthening of faith comes from
staying with it in the hour of trial.
We should not shrink from tests of faith.
Catherine Marshall

Under the Circumstances

*I'm just as happy with little as with much, with much
as with little. I've found the recipe for being happy
whether full or hungry, hands full or hands empty.
Whatever I have, wherever I am, I can make it through
anything in the One who makes me who I am.*
Philippians 4:12–13 MSG

You've probably heard it said on many occasions.
Perhaps you've even said it yourself: "I'm doing
the best I can under the circumstances." But God
has a better way. He wants you to live above your
circumstances—and with His help, you can do it.

In Philippians, the apostle Paul stated that he
could find happiness and fulfillment in any situation.
How? By turning His life and his future over to God.
Even when he faced enormous difficulties, Paul
found peace through God. So can you.

Today, make this important promise to yourself
and to your Creator: vow to rise above your
circumstances and be content in Christ. When you
trust Him to help you and to provide for your needs,
you won't have to live "under the circumstances."

*A child of God should be a visible beatitude
for happiness and a living doxology for gratitude.*
C. H. Spurgeon

The Cost of Ownership

*Since we entered the world penniless
and will leave it penniless, if we have bread on the table
and shoes on our feet, that's enough.*
1 Timothy 6:7–8 MSG

Henry David Thoreau, the iconic New England naturalist and author, is perhaps best known for his masterpiece, *Walden*. Thoreau wrote, "The cost of a thing is the amount of life that must be exchanged for it." His advice seems even more appropriate today than in the nineteenth century, when he penned it. After all, today's world is overflowing with distractions and temptations Henry David Thoreau scarcely could have imagined.

If you're buying more things but enjoying them less, perhaps it's time to simplify your life. After all, as Thoreau found through his experiment of minimalist living in a one-room cabin in the woods, sometimes less stuff can mean more happiness. And we could all afford a little more of that.

*There is absolutely no evidence that complexity and
materialism lead to happiness. On the contrary, there is
plenty of evidence that simplicity
and spirituality lead to joy, a blessedness
that is better than happiness.*
Dennis Swanberg

Forgiveness and the Golden Rule

Whatever you want others to do for you, do also the same
for them—this is the Law and the Prophets.
Matthew 7:12 HCSB

How should we treat other people? God's Word is clear: we should treat others in the same way we wish to be treated. This Golden Rule is easy to understand, but it can be difficult to live by.

Because we're imperfect human beings, we are, on occasion, selfish, thoughtless, unforgiving, or even cruel. But Jesus taught us to behave otherwise. He showed us how to treat others with mercy and compassion. When we follow in His footsteps, rising above our selfish concerns to put others first, we help to build His kingdom.

Matthew 7:12 tells us to do for others what we'd want them to do for us, and that includes forgiving them as we would want to be forgiven . . . indeed, as we have been forgiven. When we weave the thread of forgiveness into the fabric of our lives, we give glory to the One who first forgave us.

Looking back over my life, all I can see is mercy
and grace written in large letters everywhere.
May God help me have the same kind of heart toward
those who wound or offend me.
Jim Cymbala

The Rock

I will proclaim the LORD's name. Declare the greatness
of our God! The Rock—His work is perfect;
all His ways are entirely just. A faithful God,
without prejudice, He is righteous and true.
Deuteronomy 32:3–4 HCSB

God is the creator of life, the sustainer of life, and the Rock upon which victorious lives are built. He is a never-ending source of support for those who trust Him, and He is an unfailing source of wisdom for those who study His Word.

Is God the Rock upon which you've constructed your own life? If so, then you have chosen wisely. Your faith will help you to rise above the trials and struggles of life.

God will hold your hand and walk with you today and every day if you let Him. Even when your circumstances are difficult, trust the Rock. His promises remain true; His plan is perfect; His love is eternal; and His goodness endures forever.

Our heavenly Father wants nothing but the best
for any of us, and only He knows what that is,
for He is all-wise, the Omniscient.
Elisabeth Elliot

God's Guidance

*The true children of God are those
who let God's Spirit lead them.*
Romans 8:14 NCV

The Bible promises that God will guide us if we let Him. But sometimes we're tempted to let others guide us. Sometimes it seems easier to go along with the crowd; other times we'd just rather do things our way rather than God's way. When we feel those temptations, it's important that we recognize and resist them. As God's children, we must choose to be led by God's Spirit.

What or whom will you allow to guide you through the coming day: your own desires (or the desires of your friends)? Or will you let God lead the way?

When you choose God as your guide, entrusting your life to Him completely and without reservation, He will give you the strength to meet any challenge, the courage to face any trial, and the wisdom to live in His righteousness. So trust Him today and seek His guidance. When you do, you'll receive the blessings promised to His children.

God's leading will never be contrary to His Word.
Vonette Bright

Everywhere

The eyes of the LORD are in every place, keeping watch.
Proverbs 15:3 NKJV

If God is everywhere, why does He sometimes seem so far away? It's a question nearly all of us ask at some time in our lives. The answer, of course, has little to do with God and everything to do with us.

When we begin each day on our knees, in praise and worship, God often seems very near indeed. But if we ignore God or, worse yet, rebel against Him altogether, our world can feel like a spiritual wasteland.

Are you tired, discouraged, or fearful? Be comforted, knowing that God is with you. Are you confused? Listen to the quiet voice of your heavenly Father. Are you bitter? Talk with God and seek His healing. Are you celebrating a great victory? Thank God and praise Him. He is the Giver of all good things. In whatever condition you find yourself—happy or sad, victorious or vanquished, troubled or triumphant—remember that God is near, watching over you. Celebrate His presence today.

To be with God wondering, that is adoration. To be with God gratefully, that is thanksgiving. To be with God ashamed, that is contrition. To be with God with people and things we care about in our hearts, that is intercession. But the center of it, in desire and in design, will be the being with God.
Michael Ramsey, Archbishop of Canterbury

God's Sovereignty

Can you solve the mysteries of God? Can you discover
everything about the Almighty? Such knowledge is higher
than the heavens—and who are you? It is deeper than
the underworld—what do you know?
It is broader than the earth and wider than the sea.
Job 11:7–9 NLT

God is sovereign. He reigns over the entire universe, and He reigns over your little corner of that universe. The question is, do you recognize God's sovereignty, live in accordance with His commandments, and trust His promises? You know you should, of course, but sometimes these things are easier said than done.

Your heavenly Father may not always reveal Himself as quickly (or as clearly) as you would like. But rest assured: God is in control, and He wants to use you in wonderful, unexpected ways. He desires to lead you along a path of His choosing. Today, determine to watch, to listen, to learn . . . and to follow.

Waiting is the hardest kind of work,
but God knows best,
and we may joyfully leave all in His hands.
Lottie Moon

Placing Your Hope in God

LORD, I turn my hope to You. My God, I trust in You.
Psalm 25:1–2 HCSB

The hope the world promises is fleeting and imperfect. The hope God promises is unshakable and unending. It's no wonder, then, that when we seek security from worldly sources, our hopes are often dashed. But God has no such record of failure.

Where will you place your hope today? Will you entrust your future to mankind or to God? Will you seek solace exclusively from fallible human beings, or will you place your life and your heart in the trustworthy hands of your Creator?

Today, as you take the next step in your life's journey, consider these words from the psalmist: "You are my hope; O Lord GOD, You are my confidence" (Psalm 71:5 NASB). Place your hope in the One you can truly trust.

We must accept finite disappointment,
but we must never lose infinite hope.
Martin Luther King Jr.

Passing Judgment

You, therefore, have no excuse, you who pass judgment on someone else, for at whatever point you judge the other, you are condemning yourself.

Romans 2:1 NIV

The Bible tells us to resist the temptation to judge others (see Matthew 7:1). Yet even the most merciful among us may occasionally fall prey to the powerful inclination to judge.

When Jesus encountered a young woman who had been condemned by the Pharisees, religious leaders of that day, He spoke not only to the crowd that had gathered to join the condemnation but also to future generations when He warned, "He that is without sin among you, let him first cast a stone at her" (John 8:7 KJV). Jesus's message is clear, and it applies not only to the Pharisees of ancient times but also to us.

So the next time you're tempted to pass judgment on another human being, catch yourself before you make that mistake. Don't be a judge; be a witness of God's love and compassion.

Perhaps the greatest blessing that religious inheritance can bestow is an open mind, one that can listen without judging.

Kathleen Norris

God over Possessions

*No one can serve two masters. The person will hate
one master and love the other, or will follow one master
and refuse to follow the other.
You cannot serve both God and worldly riches.*
Matthew 6:24 NCV

In modern society, we need money to live. But
as thoughtful men and women who trust God's
promises, we must never make the acquisition of
money the central focus of our lives. Money is a tool,
but it should never overwhelm our sensibilities and
become an end in itself. The focus of life must be kept
squarely on spiritual things, not material things.

Anytime we place our love for material possessions
above our love for God, we find ourselves engaged
in a struggle between good and evil. Let us respond
to this struggle by freeing ourselves from that subtle
yet powerful temptation: the temptation to love the
world more than we love God.

*If you want to be truly happy,
you won't find it on an endless quest for more stuff.
You'll find it in receiving God's generosity
and in the passing that generosity along.*
Bill Hybels

Impatience

The Lord is waiting to show you mercy,
and is rising up to show you compassion, for the LORD
is a just God. Happy are all who wait patiently for Him.
Isaiah 30:18 HCSB

Are you a person in a hurry? If so, you may be in for a few disappointments. Why? Because life has a way of unfolding according to its own timetable, not yours. That's why life requires patience . . . and lots of it.

Lamentations 3:25 reminds us, "The Lord is wonderfully good to those who wait for him and seek him" (NIV). But for most of us, waiting quietly is difficult—after all, we're in a hurry for things to happen!

The next time you find your patience tested, step back; slow down, take a deep breath, and relax. Sometimes life can't be hurried—and at all times, patience is a virtue with a promise of reward.

When we read of the great biblical leaders,
we see that it was not uncommon for God to ask them
to wait, not just a day or two, but for years,
until God was ready for them to act.
Gloria Gaither

God's Peace and God's Word

If only you had paid attention to My commands. Then
your peace would have been like a river, and your
righteousness like the waves of the sea.
Isaiah 48:18 HCSB

Do you seek God's peace? Then study His Word.
The Bible is a road map for life here on earth,
with the destination of life eternal. We are called
upon to study God's Word, to trust His promises, to
follow His commandments, and to share the Good
News with the world.

The words of Matthew 4:4 remind us that we
should not "live by bread alone, but by every word that
proceeds from the mouth of God" (NKJV). If we are
to live by God's Word, we must read it and meditate
on its meaning for our lives. Otherwise we deprive
ourselves of a priceless gift from our Creator.

God's Word is a transforming, one-of-a-kind
treasure. A mere passing acquaintance with it will
be insufficient for those who truly desire to follow
God and to understand His will. Today, spend time
reading your Bible. When you pay attention to God's
Word, you'll be blessed with God's peace.

Peace is full confidence that God is Who He says He is
and that He will keep every promise in His Word.
Dorothy Harrison Pentecost

Too Much Stuff

Keep your lives free from the love of money,
and be satisfied with what you have.
Hebrews 13:5 NCV

If we trust God's promises, material possessions should play a relatively small role in our lives. Of course, we all need the basic necessities; but once we meet those needs for ourselves and our families, the piling up of possessions usually creates more problems than it solves. Our real riches are not of this world. We're never really rich until we're rich in spirit.

Martin Luther once said, "Many things I have tried to grasp and have lost. That which I have placed in God's hands I still have." His words contain wisdom for all of us: our earthly riches are transitory; only spiritual riches will last.

Do you find yourself wrapped up in the concerns of the material world? If so, perhaps it's time to reorder your priorities by turning your thoughts and energies to more important matters. Today, begin storing up riches that will endure throughout eternity.

Everything we have is God's;
we only borrow it for a time.
Rich DeVos

Giving Your Best

Each tree is known by its own fruit.
Luke 6:44 HCSB

God deserves your best. Is He getting it? Do you make an appointment with your heavenly Father each day (and keep it)? Do carve out moments to give Him your undivided attention? Or is your devotion distracted and sporadic?

When we acquire the habit of focusing our hearts and minds on God, searching out His will for our lives, He will guide our steps and bless our endeavors. But if we allow distractions to intrude and other things to take priority over our relationship with God, they will—and we'll suffer for our misplaced priorities.

Today, determine to give God your best: your best attention, your best devotion, your best effort. Meditate on God's promises, and focus on following Him. When you do, you'll be amazed at how quickly everything else comes into focus, too.

*It is important to set goals because if you do not have a plan, a goal, a direction, a purpose,
and a focus, you are not going to accomplish anything for the glory of God.*
Bill Bright

May

Real Repentance

Come back to the LORD and live!
Amos 5:6 NLT

Genuine repentance requires more than simply offering God apologies for our misdeeds. Real repentance may begin with feelings of sorrow and remorse, but it's complete only when we turn away from the sin that has distanced us from our Creator. In truth, we offer our most meaningful apologies to God not with our words but with our actions. As long as we are still engaged in sin, we may be "repenting," but we have not fully "repented."

Is there an aspect of your life that is distancing you from God? If so, ask for His forgiveness, and—just as importantly—change your behavior. Then wrap yourself in the protection of God's promises. When you do, you can truly live.

In terms of the parable of the Prodigal Son,
repentance is the flight home that leads
to joyful celebration. It opens the way to a future,
to a relationship restored.
Philip Yancey

The Power of Silence

*Truly my soul silently waits for God;
from Him comes my salvation.*
Psalm 62:1 NKJV

The world seems to grow louder day by day, and sometimes it seems our senses are assaulted at every turn. But if we allow the distractions of a clamorous society to separate us from God's peace, we do ourselves a profound disservice. Instead, in a world filled with noise, we must carve out moments of silence.

If we are to maintain righteous minds and compassionate hearts, we must take time each day for prayer and for meditation on God's Word. We must make ourselves still in the presence of our Creator. We must quiet our minds and our hearts so that we can sense God's will and be enveloped by His love.

Has the busy pace of life robbed you of the peace God has promised? If so, find time today to be still and reclaim the inner peace that can be found in the silent moments you spend with God.

God is the friend of silence. See how nature—trees, flowers, grass—grows in silence; see the stars, the moon and the sun, how they move in silence.
We need silence to be able to touch souls.
Mother Teresa

Defining Success

If you do not stand firm in your faith,
then you will not stand at all.
Isaiah 7:9 HCSB

How do you define success? Do you see it as the accumulation of material possessions or the adulation of your neighbors? If so, perhaps it's time to take a second look. Genuine success has little to do with fame or fortune; it has everything to do with God's gift of love and His promise of salvation.

If you have welcomed God into your heart, you already are a towering success; but there's still more that you can do. As a person who has received God's grace, your next step is to stand firm in that faith—and to lay hold of the spiritual abundance and peace He offers to those who trust His promises. Then you can share the healing message of God's love and the hope of His promises with a world that desperately needs both. When you do, you'll know the sweetness of success in God's eyes.

We . . . must allow God to define success.
And, when we do, God blesses us
with His love and His grace.
Jim Gallery

Focusing on Your Hopes

This hope we have as an anchor of the soul,
both sure and steadfast, and which enters
the Presence behind the veil.
Hebrews 6:19 NKJV

French poet and philosopher Paul Valéry once observed, "We hope vaguely but dread precisely." All too often, we allow the worries of everyday life to overshadow our thoughts and cloud our vision. What we need is a clearer perspective, renewed faith, and a different focus.

When we focus on the frustrations of today or the uncertainties of tomorrow, we rob ourselves of peace in the present. But when we focus on God's grace, and when we trust in the ultimate wisdom of God's plan for our lives, our worries will no longer tyrannize us.

Today, remember that God is infinitely greater than the challenges you face. Focus your hopes on Him, and you'll have reason for hope indeed.

The essence of optimism is that it takes no account of the
present, but it is a source of inspiration,
of vitality, and of hope. Where others have resigned, it
enables a man to hold his head high, to claim the future
for himself, and not abandon it to his enemy.
Dietrich Bonhoeffer

Actions That Speak Loudly

*Are there those among you who are truly wise
and understanding? Then they should show it by living
right and doing good things with a gentleness
that comes from wisdom.*
James 3:13 NCV

The old saying is both familiar and true: actions speak louder than words. So we should always make sure our actions reflect the positive changes God can make in the lives of those who walk with Him.

The Creator calls upon each of us to act in accordance with His will and with respect for His commandments. It's never enough simply to hear God's instructions; we must also follow them. And it's never enough to wait idly by while others do the Father's work here on earth; we, too, must act.

Doing God's work is a responsibility each of us must bear; but when we do, our loving, heavenly Father promises to reward our efforts with a bountiful harvest in this world and in the next.

*You cannot spell God or Gospel
until you first spell "go."*
Anonymous

Reasons to Rejoice

Keep your eyes focused on what is right,
and look straight ahead to what is good.
Proverbs 4:25 NCV

In light of the many wonderful promises in the Bible, we have every reason to rejoice. God is in His heaven; His Son has risen to provide forgiveness and reconciliation, and dawn has broken on another day of life. Yet sometimes, when the burdens of life seem heavy, you may find yourself feeling exhausted, discouraged, or both. That's when you need a fresh supply of hope . . . and God is ready, willing, and able to supply it.

The advice in Proverbs 4:5 is clear-cut: focus on what is good. In other words, strive to maintain a positive, can-do attitude.

As you face the challenges of the coming day, use God's Word as a tool for directing your thoughts. When you do, your attitude will be pleasing to God, pleasing to your friends, and pleasing to yourself. And that's just one more reason to rejoice.

Your attitude, not your aptitude,
will determine your altitude.
Zig Ziglar

Celebrating God's Gifts

Rejoice, and be exceeding glad:
for great is your reward in heaven.
Matthew 5:12 KJV

D o you celebrate the gifts God has given you? Do you rejoice in the beauty of God's glorious creation? You should. But perhaps, as a busy person living in a demanding world, you've been too distracted to count your gifts and so busy that you don't slow down long enough to offer thanks to the Giver.

As God's children, we all are blessed beyond measure, and we should celebrate those blessings every day that we live. Today is a nonrenewable resource—once it's gone, it's gone forever. So as thoughtful adults, let's give thanks for God's gifts . . . and then use them in the service of His people.

God has blessed us abundantly, and we owe Him everything, including our praise. Knowing that we've been promised a great reward in heaven should spur us to celebrate God's gifts here on earth.

All our life is a celebration for us; we are convinced, in
fact, that God is always everywhere.
We sing while we work . . . we pray while we
carry out all life's other occupations.
Saint Clement of Alexandria

Comforting Others

Blessed be the God and Father of our Lord Jesus Christ,
the Father of mercies and the God of all comfort.
He comforts us in all our affliction, so that we may be
able to comfort those who are in any kind of affliction,
through the comfort we ourselves receive from God.
2 Corinthians 1:3–4 HCSB

God comforts us, and He asks us to comfort others—but our heavenly Father doesn't stop there. He also gives us countless opportunities to offer encouragement to our family members, to our friends, and even to complete strangers. When we do, we spread the seeds of hope and happiness, and the Father smiles upon our endeavors.

Today, when you encounter someone who needs a helping hand or a comforting word, be generous with both. God has instilled in you the ability to make the world a better place one person—and one hug—at a time. When you use that power wisely, you make your own corner of the world a kinder, gentler, happier place.

Nothing opens the heart like a true friend, to whom you
may impart griefs, joys, fears, hopes, suspicions, counsels,
and whatever lies upon the heart.
Francis Bacon

Facing Difficult Days

We are pressured in every way but not crushed;
we are perplexed but not in despair.
2 Corinthians 4:8 HCSB

All of us face difficult days. Sometimes even the most faith-filled folks can become discouraged, and you're no exception. After all, you live in a world where expectations can be high . . . and demands can be even higher.

If you find yourself sagging under the weight of heavy burdens or difficult circumstances, remember that God is a ready source of strength. If you become discouraged with the direction of your day or your life, turn your thoughts and prayers to Him. He is a God of possibility, not negativity, so don't despair. He will guide you and bring you safely through your difficulties. And then, with a renewed spirit of optimism and hope, you can give thanks to the Giver of all good things . . . and you'll know that in the future, you can face even the most difficult of days with His help.

When life is difficult, God wants us to have
a faith that trusts and waits.
Kay Arthur

A Beacon of Encouragement

Encourage each other. Live in harmony and peace.
Then the God of love and peace will be with you.
2 Corinthians 13:11 NLT

One of the reasons God placed you here on earth is so that you might be a beacon of encouragement to others. As a child of God, you have every reason to be hopeful—so why not share that hope with others? After all, optimism, hope, and cheerfulness, like other human emotions, are contagious.

Today and every day, look for the good in others, and celebrate the good you find. Be quick to offer a smile, a hug, a kind word, or all three. When you do, you'll quickly discover that one of the surest ways to cheer yourself up is by trying your best to cheer up somebody else.

Giving encouragement to others is a most
welcome gift, for the results of it are lifted spirits,
increased self-worth, and a hopeful future.
Florence Littauer

Focusing on God

Give your entire attention to what God is doing right now, and don't get worked up about what may or may not happen tomorrow. God will help you deal with whatever hard things come up when the time comes.

Matthew 6:34 MSG

All of us, at one time or another, find our courage tested by the disappointments and tragedies of life. There's no avoiding the reality that the world is filled with uncertainty, hardship, sickness, and danger. Trouble, it seems, is never far from the door.

When we focus on our fears and our doubts, we'll find many reasons to lie awake at night, fretting about the uncertainties of the coming day. But if we discipline ourselves to focus on God instead of on our fears about what might happen tomorrow, we'll not only get a better night's sleep; we'll also be better able to face the actual events of tomorrow.

God is as near as your next breath, and He is in control. He is your shield and your strength; He will help you if you ask Him to. So don't dwell on your doubts. Trust God's plan and depend on His promises.

Do not fear what may happen tomorrow.
The same loving Father who cares for you today
will care for you tomorrow and every day.

Saint Francis de Sales

Forgiveness

*Anyone who claims to live in God's light
and hates a brother or sister is still in the dark.*
1 John 2:9 MSG

Forgiveness is seldom easy, but it's always right.
When we forgive those who have hurt us, we
honor God. But when we harbor bitterness against
others, we disobey God—with predictably unhappy
results.

Are you easily frustrated by the shortcomings of
others? Are you a prisoner of bitterness or regret? Do
you hold on to a grudge a little longer (or maybe a lot
longer) than you should? If so, maybe it's time for a
refresher course in the art of forgiveness.

If you're having a hard time forgiving someone
(and that includes yourself), pray about it. Ask God
to heal your wounds and to help you extend to others
the kind of forgiveness He has extended to you. The
world is a dark enough place. Do your part to shine
the light of God's forgiveness.

*It is better to forgive and forget
than to resent and remember.*
Barbara Johnson

Generosity

Be generous: Invest in acts of charity.
Charity yields high returns.
Ecclesiastes 11:1 MSG

God's Word promises a reward for generosity. So if we want to experience the fullness of God's blessings, we must be generous with our time, our talents, our encouragement, and our possessions. When we become generous ambassadors for God, He will bless us in even more wonderful ways than we can anticipate. But if we allow ourselves to become closefisted and miserly with our possessions, our time, our abilities, or our love, we deprive ourselves of the spiritual abundance that could otherwise be ours.

Do you seek God's promised abundance and peace? Then share with others the blessings He has given you. You'll find that when you do, even the many blessings you now have will be multiplied . . . and so will your joy.

If we can learn to develop a giving heart toward those in our own homes and families, we'll be much more free to give ungrudgingly—and at the Spirit's prompting—to those in the most desperate need.
Mary Hunt

God's Correction

Do not reject the LORD's discipline,
and don't get angry when he corrects you.
Proverbs 3:11 NCV

When we stray from God's path, He mercifully finds ways to correct us. When our behavior is inconsistent with God's will, our heavenly Father disciplines us in much the same way as a loving parent might discipline a wayward child. God corrects us because He loves us, and if we're wise, we'll accept His correction and learn from it.

The Bible teaches us that when God corrects us, we should accept His discipline without bitterness or despair (see Hebrews 12:5). Instead of bemoaning our fate, we should look upon God's instruction as an occasion to repair our mistakes, to reorder our priorities, and to realign our lives with His perfect plan.

God's correction is purposeful: He's trying to draw us back into the safety and comfort of His loving arms. Today, let us accept His kind discipline and consider it an opportunity to change, to learn, and to grow.

God is a God of unconditional, unremitting love,
a love that corrects and chastens but never ceases.
Kay Arthur

The God of Love

God is love, and the one who remains in love remains in God, and God remains in him.

1 John 4:16 HCSB

God is love. It's a sweeping statement, a profoundly important description of what God is and how God works. God's love is perfect, and it's powerful: when we open our hearts to His love, we are transformed.

Today, even if you can only carve out a few moments of quiet time, offer sincere prayers of thanksgiving to your heavenly Father. Thank Him for His promise of love and for His many blessings. As you sit in silence, open your heart to sense His presence, and open your ears to hear His voice. When you do, you'll be enveloped in the genuine love that flows from the loving heart of God. You can experience true love today . . . simply open your heart to the God of love.

The great love of God
is an ocean without a bottom or a shore.
C. H. Spurgeon

God's Will for You

This world is fading away, along with everything
that people crave. But anyone who does
what pleases God will live forever.
1 John 2:17 NLT

As human beings with limited understanding, we can never fully comprehend the will of God. But as believers in a benevolent God, we must always trust the will of our heavenly Father.

Before His crucifixion, Jesus went to the Mount of Olives and poured out His heart to God (see Luke 22:41–44). Jesus knew that He was about to suffer agony and death, but He also knew that God's will must be done.

In our own lives, we will face trials that bring fear and trembling to the very depths of our souls. But like Jesus, we, too, must seek God's will, not our own.

Today, seek God's will for your life, and trust His promises. When you do, you will be blessed today, tomorrow, for every day of your life . . . and for eternity.

Life isn't life without some divine decisions
that our mortal minds simply cannot comprehend.
Beth Moore

Too Wise to Be Jealous

*Where jealousy and selfishness are,
there will be confusion and every kind of evil.*
James 3:16 NCV

Are you too wise to be consumed by feelings of jealousy?

Jesus taught us to love our neighbors, not to envy them. But sometimes, despite our best intentions, we fall prey to feelings of jealousy, and envy. Why? Because we're human, and because we live in a world that places great importance on material possessions. But to focus on those possessions is shortsighted and unwise. Those aren't the things that matter to God, so we shouldn't allow them to take precedence in our lives.

The next time you feel pangs of envy, remind yourself of two things: (1) jealousy and selfishness never generate anything good; and (2) God has already showered you with so many blessings that as a thoughtful, thankful person, you already know it's far better to focus on those than to let jealousy of others distort your view and torture your soul.

*The jealous are troublesome to others,
but a torment to themselves.*
William Penn

Preparing for Today . . .
and for Eternity

The last enemy that will be destroyed is death.
1 Corinthians 15:26 NKJV

It's imperative to be fully engaged in life, but it's also imperative to prepare for the end of life. Physical death, after all, is an inevitability for all of us. And the seasons of life turn quickly—too quickly, in fact—for a single day to be wasted.

Life is a glorious opportunity, but it is a shockingly brief one. So we should treat each day as a precious gift, and we should serve God each day as if it were our last day.

Today is a priceless gift from the Father above. So trust His promise of eternal life, and then dive into the thick of life here on earth by living courageously and purposefully. When you do, you'll make this day yet another victory for the One who has already given you so much—the One who still has so much to give.

To be prepared to die is to be prepared to live;
to be ready for eternity is, in the best sense,
to be ready for today.
C. H. Spurgeon

The Wisdom of Moderation

Moderation is better than muscle,
self-control better than political power.
Proverbs 16:32 MSG

Moderation and wisdom are traveling companions. If we're wise, we will learn to temper our appetites, our desires, and our impulses. When we do, we'll be blessed—in part, because God has created a world in which temperance is rewarded and intemperance brings undesirable consequences.

Would you like to improve your life? Then harness your appetites and restrain your compulsions. Moderation is difficult, yes; it's especially difficult in a prosperous and indulgent society such as ours. But the rewards of moderation are numerous and long-lasting. Choose to pursue those rewards today.

No one can force you to moderate your appetites. The decision to live temperately is yours and yours alone. But it's the wise way to live, and it's the path to God's promised blessings.

Perhaps too much of everything
is as bad as too little.
Edna Ferber

Giving Up

It is better to finish something than to start it.
It is better to be patient than to be proud.
Ecclesiastes 7:8 NCV

Occasional disappointments, detours, and failures are inevitable, even for the most accomplished among us. Setbacks are simply the price we sometimes pay for our willingness to take risks as we pursue our dreams. But we must never allow these hardships to cause us to lose faith.

American children's rights advocate Marian Wright Edelman asked, "Whoever said anybody has a right to give up?" That's a question we should ask ourselves, especially when times get tough.

Are you willing to keep fighting the good fight even when you meet with difficulties? If you'll decide to press on through temporary setbacks, you may be pleasantly surprised at the creative ways God finds to help determined people like you—people who possess the wisdom and the courage to persevere.

Failure is one of life's most powerful teachers.
How we handle our failures determines
whether we're going to simply
"get by" in life or "press on."
Beth Moore

Everyday Worship

Every day will I bless thee;
and I will praise thy name for ever and ever.
Psalm 145:2 KJV

Praise for our Creator shouldn't be reserved for mealtimes, or bedtimes, or church services. Rather, we should praise God all day, every day, to the greatest extent we can—with thanksgiving in our hearts and a song on our lips.

Worship can and should be woven into the fabric of every day, not just Sunday. Well-known preacher A. W. Tozer once said, "If you will not worship God seven days a week, you do not worship Him on one day a week."

So today, find time to lift your prayers to God and thank Him for all He has done. Every time you notice a gift from the Giver of good things, praise Him. His works are marvelous, His gifts are bountiful, and His love endures forever.

Two wings are necessary to lift our souls toward God:
prayer and praise.
Prayer asks. Praise accepts the answer.
Mrs. Charles E. Cowman

At Peace with Your Purpose

The LORD will work out his plans for my life—
for your faithful love, O LORD, endures forever.
Psalm 138:8 NLT

A re you at peace with the direction of your life?
You can be if you entrust your life to God. Even
when you don't know or understand God's plans
for you, you can rest in the knowledge that His
love for you is certain. And because God keeps His
promises, you can be sure that He is working out
His plan for your life.

When you welcome God's love into your heart,
your life will be transformed. The Father's peace will
become yours, and then, because you possess the gift
of peace, you can share that gift with family members,
with friends, and with coworkers.

Today offers yet another opportunity to welcome
the Creator into your heart and share His Good
News with the world. It's the right thing to do—and
when you do the right thing, you'll always be at peace
with your purpose.

When we realize and embrace the Lord's will for us, we
will love to do it. We won't want
to do anything else. It's a passion.
Franklin Graham

Embraced by the Father

The faithful love of the LORD never ends!
Lamentations 3:22 NLT

Every day of your life—indeed, every moment of your life—you are embraced by God. He is always with you, and His love for you is deeper and more profound than you can comprehend.

Precisely because you are a wondrous creation treasured by God, a question presents itself: what will you do in response to God's love? Will you accept it or reject it? Will you return it or neglect it? The decision is yours and yours alone.

When you open yourself to God's love, you'll feel differently about yourself, your neighbors, and your world. When you embrace your heavenly Father, you'll share His message and strive to obey His instructions.

When you accept the Father's grace and share His love with others, you will be blessed here on earth and throughout all eternity. Accept His love today.

As the sun shines on all things on earth in the same way, yet as if each is separate, that is how God's love is for each of us: the same yet unique.
Saint Thérèse de Lisieux

Spiritual Gifts

Pursue love and desire spiritual gifts.
1 Corinthians 14:1 HCSB

Have you given much thought to your spiritual gifts? Whether you realize it or not, you have a surprising array of God-given talents that you can use to honor Him and build His kingdom.

How will you use your spiritual gifts? Will you humbly ask God to use you as an instrument of His will, and will you prayerfully ask Him to use your talents for His glory and His purposes? If you do, God has promised to guide your steps and answer your prayers.

So today, ask God to use all your talents—spiritual and otherwise—to improve His world and yours. When you do, God will use you and bless you . . . and no other pursuit in life can promise a greater joy.

We are born to make manifest the glory of God
that is within us. It is not just in some of us;
it is in everyone. As we let our own light shine,
we unconsciously give other people
permission to do the same.
Nelson Mandela

Giving Thanks to the Creator

I will give You thanks with all my heart.
Psalm 138:1 HCSB

Most of us have been blessed beyond measure; yet sometimes, as busy people living in a demanding world, we get distracted and neglect to give the thanks we owe to our Creator.

Are you determined to be a thankful recipient of God's gifts? Are you unwavering in your commitment to praise God many times each day?

Your heavenly Father has promised to bless you, to protect you, and to lead you along a path of His choosing. As the old saying goes, "When you drink the water, you should remember the spring." So today, slow down enough to recognize and appreciate God's blessings. His love for you is never-ending, so it's always the right time to give Him the thanks He so richly deserves.

The unthankful heart discovers no mercies;
but the thankful heart will find, in every hour,
some heavenly blessings!
Henry Ward Beecher

Trusting the All-Powerful God

*Through your faith, God is protecting you by his power
until you receive this salvation.*
1 Peter 1:5 NLT

Sometimes the future seems bright . . . and sometimes it doesn't. Yet even when we cannot see the possibilities of tomorrow, God can. Our challenge, then, is to trust an uncertain future to an all-powerful God.

When we trust God, we should trust Him without reservation. We should steel ourselves against the various disappointments of the day, secure in the knowledge that our heavenly Father has a plan for the future that only He can see but that is for our good.

Can you place your future into the hands of a loving and all-knowing God? Can you live amid the uncertainties of today, knowing that God has dominion over all your tomorrows? If you can, you are wise—and you will be blessed.

*We shall steer safely through every storm, as long as our
heart is right, our intention fervent,
our courage steadfast, and our trust fixed in God.*
Saint Francis de Sales

God's Unchanging Wisdom

Joyful is the person who finds wisdom,
the one who gains understanding.
Proverbs 3:13 NLT

Sometimes, amid the concerns of everyday life, we lose perspective. Life seems out of balance as we confront an array of demands that sap our strength and cloud our thinking. At such times we need a fresh dose of God's wisdom.

Here in the twenty-first century, commentary is commonplace and information is everywhere. But the ultimate source of wisdom, the kind of timeless wisdom that God willingly shares with His children, is still available from a single, unique source: the Bible.

The wisdom of the world changes with the ever-shifting sands of public opinion. God's wisdom is eternal. It never changes, because it's always right. And that's the wisdom that we must use to plan our day, our life, and our eternal destiny.

Consider seriously how quickly people change,
and how little trust is to be had in them;
and hold fast to God, who does not change.
Saint Teresa of Avila

The Treasure Hunt

Where your treasure is, there will your heart be also.
Luke 12:34 KJV

All of mankind is engaged in a colossal, worldwide treasure hunt. Some people seek treasure from earthly sources—trinkets of material wealth or public acclaim. Others seek spiritual treasures by making God the cornerstone of their lives.

What kind of treasure hunter are you? Are you so caught up in the demands of everyday living that you sometimes allow the search for worldly treasures to become your primary focus? If so, take a few moments today to reorganize your to-do list, placing God in His rightful place: first place. Don't allow anyone or anything to separate you from your heavenly Father.

The world's treasures are difficult to find and impossible, ultimately, to keep; God's treasures are available to all who seek Him, and they are everlasting.

I have a divided heart, trying to love God
and the world at the same time. God says,
"You can't love me as you should
if you love this world too."
Mary Morrison Suggs

Excited about Opportunities

May the God of hope fill you with all joy and peace as
you trust in him, so that you may overflow
with hope by the power of the Holy Spirit.
Romans 15:13 NIV

The world is brimming with possibilities. Have you noticed? Are you genuinely excited about the opportunities God has placed along your path? You should be! After all, God has promised to do wonderful things in you and through you . . . but He does expect you to do your share of the work. Each morning, God presents you with a world full of opportunities. Will you make good use of them?

Sometime today, if you pay careful attention, you'll see an exciting opportunity God has placed along your path. Perhaps it will be disguised as a problem. Maybe it will masquerade as hard work. No matter. Even if your opportunity is difficult to recognize and even more difficult to seize, with God's help you can make the most of it. He's willing. Are you?

Those who are fired with an enthusiastic idea and who
allow it to take hold and dominate their thoughts find
that new worlds open for them. As long as enthusiasm
holds out, so will new opportunities.
Norman Vincent Peale

Holiness before Happiness

*Whoever keeps His word, truly in him the love
of God is perfected. This is how we know we are in Him:
the one who says he remains in Him
should walk just as He walked.*
1 John 2:5–6 HCSB

As an imperfect human being, you're probably not "perfectly" happy. But did you know that's perfectly okay with God? He is far less concerned with your happiness than He is with your holiness.

God continuously reveals Himself in everyday life, but He does not do so in order to make us contented; He does so in order to lead us to Him. Some days drawing closer to God is easy and pleasant. Some days it can be difficult and uncomfortable. But draw closer we must. So don't be overly concerned with your current level of happiness: it will change. Be more concerned with the current state of your relationship with the Creator: He will never change. And in the end, if we walk closely with Him, His joy will become our joy . . . for all eternity.

*His goal is not necessarily to make us happy.
His goal is to make us His.*
Kathy Troccoli

Making Time for God

*Blessed are they which do hunger
and thirst after righteousness:
for they shall be filled.*
Matthew 5:6 KJV

When it comes to spending time with God, are you a squeezer or a pleaser? Do you squeeze God into your schedule, with an occasional prayer before meals, or do you please God by talking to Him far more often than that? Wise people form the habit of spending time with God every day. They know that doing so will change the quality and the direction of their lives. They understand that the more time they spend with God, the more they will experience His abundance, His peace, and His love.

Even if your to-do list is filled with a string of urgent obligations, you can still carve out a few quiet moments each day to spend with your Creator. When you think about all the things God has done for you, making time for Him seems not only the right thing to do, but the best thing.

*Half an hour of listening to God is essential
except when one is very busy.
Then, a full hour is needed.*
Saint Francis de Sales

June

Beyond Panic

When my anxious thoughts multiply within me,
Your consolations delight my soul.
Psalm 94:19 NASB

We live in a world that seems to invite panic. Everywhere we turn, we're confronted with disturbing images that seem to cry out, "All is lost." But with God, there's always hope.

God enables us, indeed calls us, to live above anxiety. He created us to live by faith, not by fear. He instructs us to trust Him completely, this day and forever. But sometimes trusting God feels difficult, especially when we get caught up in the incessant demands and worries of an anxious world.

When you feel anxious—and you will—turn your thoughts to God and remember His love. Take your concerns to Him in prayer and, to the best of your ability, leave them there. God is capable of handling any problem you turn over to Him, and He has promised to comfort and help you, if you'll just trust Him.

Quiet minds cannot be perplexed or frightened,
but go on in fortune or misfortune at their own private
pace, like a clock during a thunderstorm.
Robert Louis Stevenson

Surrounded with Favor

Surely, O LORD, you bless the righteous;
you surround them with your favor as with a shield.
Psalm 5:12 NIV

God blesses and protects those who live righteously and honorably—and that's a promise you can depend on. If you do your part (by living in accordance with God's teachings), He will most certainly do His part (by showering you with blessings in this world and the next).

Do you sincerely believe that God is on your side? Do you trust Him when He promises to love and protect you? Are you willing to seek God's guidance and follow His lead, wherever it may take you? If you can answer these questions with a clear and resounding yes, then your heavenly Father will surround you with His favor and be your Shield. He will bless you and keep you now and forever . . . just as He has promised.

The promises of Scripture are not mere pious hopes or
sanctified guesses. They are more than sentimental
words to be printed on decorated cards for Sunday-school
children. They are eternal verities.
They are true. There is no perhaps about them.
Peter Marshall

Finishing the Work

*Even while we were with you, we gave you this command:
"Those unwilling to work will not get to eat."*
2 Thessalonians 3:10 NLT

William James was the son of a noted theologian, brother of a great novelist, and himself a Harvard professor and one of the founding fathers of American psychology. James was also a commonsense philosopher who once observed, "Nothing is so fatiguing as the hanging on of an uncompleted task." The professor's advice was spot on.

All of us are tempted sometimes to postpone the unpleasant. But giving in to that temptation just allows minor problems to mushroom into full-blown crises. That why it's always better to tackle problems when they're in their infancy.

So today, make a promise to yourself that you'll finish any unfinished work (even if it's unpleasant) before you begin something else. After all, as Professor James would be quick to point out, the best place to put trouble is behind you. Class dismissed.

All that is necessary to break the spell of inertia and frustration is this: act as if it were impossible to fail. That is . . . the command of right-about-face which turns us from failure towards success.
Dorothea Brande

Living Courageously

Do not fear, for I am with you; do not be dismayed,
for I am your God.
I will strengthen you and help you;
I will uphold you with my righteous right hand.
Isaiah 41:10 NIV

In light of God's many and wonderful promises, you have every reason to live courageously. He promises to protect you today and forever. God's Word promises that His love for you is never ending. But even as a person who trusts God's promises, on some days you may find your courage tested by various disappointments and fears.

When you're worried about the challenges of today or the uncertainties of tomorrow, pause and ask yourself whether you're ready to surrender your concerns and place your life in God's all-powerful, all-knowing, all-loving hands. If the answer to that question is yes, then you can draw courage today from the source of strength that never fails: your heavenly Father.

There is a living God; he has spoken in the Bible.
He means what he says and will do all he has promised.
Hudson Taylor

Beyond Your Hardships

He gives power to the weak,
and to those who have no might He increases strength.
Isaiah 40:29 NKJV

When we fail to meet the expectations of others (or, for that matter, the expectations we've set for ourselves), we may be tempted to abandon hope. Yet even on those cloudy days when our strength is sapped and our faith is shaken, there exists a God from whom we can draw courage and wisdom.

The words of Isaiah 40:31 contain a promise: "Those who wait on the LORD shall renew their strength; they shall mount up with wings like eagles, they shall run and not be weary, they shall walk and not faint" (NKJV).

So if you're feeling defeated or discouraged, instead of giving up or giving in, wait . . . on the Lord, that is. Spend time in His presence, meditating on His Word. And take this advice from Mrs. Charles E. Cowman: "Never yield to gloomy anticipation. Place your hope and confidence in God. He has no record of failure." The God who never fails will help you get beyond your hardships.

You are justified in avoiding people who send you from
their presence with less hope and strength to cope with
life's problems than when you met them.
Ella Wheeler Wilcox

Encouraging Words
for Family and Friends

Do not let any unwholesome talk come out
of your mouths, but only what is helpful for building
others up according to their needs,
that it may benefit those who listen.
Ephesians 4:29 NIV

Life is a team sport, and all of us need occasional pats on the back from our teammates.

Whether you realize it or not, many people with whom you come in contact every day are in desperate need of a hug or a smile or an encouraging word. The world can be a difficult place, and we all have friends and family members who may be troubled by the challenges of everyday life. Since we don't always know who needs our help, the best strategy is to try to encourage all the people who cross our path.

Today, do yourself and your friends a favor: be a world-class source of encouragement to everyone you meet. Never has the need been greater.

My special friends, who know me so well
and love me anyway, give me
daily encouragement to keep on.
Emilie Barnes

Facing Your Fears

They won't be afraid of bad news;
their hearts are steady because they trust the LORD.
Psalm 112:7 NCV

D o you prefer to face your fears rather than run from them? If you place your trust in God, you'll be able to do just that. God's Word tells us that when we put our trust in Him, our hearts will be steady and we won't be afraid. We'll be able to live courageously.

When the apostle Paul wrote to Timothy, he encouraged his young protégé by saying that the God they served was a bold God and that God's spirit empowered His children with boldness, too. Like Timothy, we face times of uncertainty and fear. But God's message is the same to us, today, as it was to Timothy: we can live boldly because the Spirit of God resides in us.

So today, as you face your fears, remember that God is with you, and you need not be afraid. Let Him steady your heart.

Walk boldly and wisely.
There is a hand above that will help thee on.
Philip James Bailey

Forgiveness and Renewal

Whenever you stand praying, if you have anything against anyone, forgive him, so that your Father in heaven will also forgive you your wrongdoing.
Mark 11:25 HCSB

Bitterness saps our energy; genuine forgiveness renews the spirit. If you're feeling tired, discouraged, or worse, could it be that you need to ask God to help you forgive others (just as He has already forgiven you)?

God wants His children to lead joyous lives filled with abundance and peace. But sometimes abundance and peace seem far removed from us. It's in these dark moments that we should turn to God for renewal; when we do, He will restore us, but we must be willing to forgive those who have wronged us.

Are you embittered about the past? Turn your heart toward God in prayer. Do you sincerely want to forgive someone? Ask God to help you. You'll discover that the Creator of the universe can heal every heart, including yours.

Forgiveness is actually the best revenge because it not only sets us free from the person we forgive, but it frees us to move into all that God has in store for us.
Stormie Omartian

When We Cannot Understand

"My thoughts are not your thoughts,
neither are your ways my ways," declares the LORD.
"As the heavens are higher than the earth, so are my ways
higher than your ways and my thoughts than your thoughts."
Isaiah 55:8–9 NIV

Try though we might, we cannot fully understand God's ways. We can see His handiwork and we can feel His presence, but we lack the capacity to comprehend a being of infinite power and infinite love. Someday we will understand Him completely, but until then we must trust Him completely.

Life leads us over many peaks and through many valleys. When we reach the mountaintops, we find it easy to praise God, to trust Him, and to give thanks. But while we're trudging through the dark valleys of despair, trusting God may be more difficult.

When our faith is tested, we must remember that God rules both the mountaintops and the valleys—with limitless wisdom and unchanging love—and if we trust Him, even when we cannot understand Him, He will lead us safely through.

God can see clearly no matter how dark or foggy the night
is. Trust His Word to guide you safely home.
Lisa Whelchel

Following Instructions

You will teach me how to live a holy life.
Being with you will fill me with joy; at your right hand
I will find pleasure forever.
Psalm 16:11 NCV

When we spend time with God, He will instruct us in the way we should go. God is always willing to teach, and we should always be willing to learn. But sometimes we're tempted to ignore God's instruction. If you're feeling that temptation today, resist it. Instead of ignoring God, start praying about your situation . . . and start listening to His teaching.

When we offer sincere prayers to our heavenly Father, He will give direction and meaning to our lives—but He won't force us to follow Him. God has given us the free will—we choose whether to follow His instructions . . . or not.

When we genuinely and humbly seek God's guidance, He will speak to our hearts and lead us on the path of His choosing. It's the best path for all mankind, and it's the right path for you. Follow it today.

God does not give us everything we want,
but He does fulfill all His promises as He leads us along
the best and straightest paths to Himself.
Dietrich Bonhoeffer

Setting Aside Quiet Moments

The LORD is with you when you are with Him.
If you seek Him, He will be found by you.
2 Chronicles 15:2 HCSB

Since God is everywhere, we are free to enjoy His presence whenever we take time to quiet our souls and turn our thoughts and prayers to Him. But sometimes, amid the flurry of demands that fill our days, our thoughts wander far from God. If we don't discipline ourselves to keep our focus on Him, we'll miss out on the blessings that are found only in His presence.

Do you set aside quiet moments each day to commune with your Creator? Silence is a gift that you give to yourself and to God, as an act of worship. During those precious moments of stillness, you can sense the infinite love and power of your heavenly Father—and He, in turn, will speak directly to your heart. So listen to Him today . . . and every day of your life.

People see God every day;
they just don't recognize Him.
Pearl Bailey

Your Protector

The LORD is my rock and my fortress and my deliverer;
the God of my strength, in whom I will trust.
2 Samuel 22:2–3 NKJV

You know firsthand that life isn't always easy. But as a recipient of God's blessings, you also know that throughout your life you have been protected by a loving, heavenly Father. And He is still protecting you.

In times of trouble, God is neither distant nor disinterested. To the contrary, God is always present and always engaged in the events of your life. Reach out to Him, and build your future on the Rock that cannot be shaken; trust in God and rely upon His promises. He can provide everything you really need . . . and much, much more. All you need do is open your arms and your heart to Him. Then let Him do the rest.

Kept by His power—that is the only safety.
Oswald Chambers

God's Offer of Hope

*Be of good courage, and He shall strengthen your heart,
all you who hope in the LORD.*
Psalm 31:24 NKJV

If we place our faith in God's promises, we should never lose hope. After all, God is good; His love endures; and He has promised those who follow Him the gift of eternal life—and God always keeps His promises. But sometimes even those of us who truly trust God can become discouraged.

Have you recently endured a great difficulty or suffered a life-changing loss? Are you struggling with questions for which you find no answers? Have you come close to abandoning hope? If so, now is the time to focus your thoughts—and your prayers—on God's love and His promises.

Your heavenly Father has a plan for your life—a plan that is good. So today, accept God's offer of hope, strength, and courage by putting your trust in Him. With God, your future is secure.

*In those desperate times when we feel like we don't have
an ounce of strength, He will gently pick up our heads so
that our eyes can behold something—something that will
keep His hope alive in us.*
Kathy Troccoli

Genuine Joy

The LORD reigns; let the earth rejoice.
Psalm 97:1 NKJV

When is the best time to rejoice? The present moment is always an appropriate one—now is always the right time to praise God with joy in your heart and a prayer of thanksgiving on your lips.

Are you determined to make this day a cause for celebration? Are you willing to pray for the wisdom to celebrate God's gifts? If so, the Father will hear your prayers, and He will answer them.

The Creator has filled this day with more blessings—and more opportunities—than you can count. Your challenge, of course, is to count as many as you can . . . and to get busy taking full advantage of them. Since this is the day the Lord has made, embrace it and let Him fill you with genuine joy. Then rejoice!

Joy is the serious business of heaven.
C. S. Lewis

God at Work

You are the God who works wonders;
You revealed Your strength among the peoples.
Psalm 77:14 HCSB

Do you believe that God is at work in the world? Do you also believe that nothing is impossible for Him? If so, then you know that God is perfectly capable of doing things that you, as a mere human being with limited vision and limited understanding, would deem utterly impossible. And that's precisely what God does.

Since the moment God created our universe out of nothingness, He has made a habit of doing miraculous things—and He still works miracles today. Expect God to work miracles in your own life. With God, absolutely nothing is impossible, so be watching for an amazing assortment of miracles that He stands ready, willing, and able to perform for you and yours.

All the things of the universe are perfect miracles,
each as profound as any.
Walt Whitman

Listen

Listen for God's voice in everything you do, everywhere you go; he's the one who will keep you on track.

Proverbs 3:6 MSG

Proverbs 3:6 contains this promise: if you acknowledge God's sovereignty over every aspect of your life, He will guide your path.

Today, as you prayerfully consider the path God intends for you to take, here are some things you should do: Study His Word and be ever-watchful for His signs. Associate with people who will encourage your spiritual growth. Listen carefully to that still, small voice of God's Spirit that speaks to you in the quiet moments of your daily devotional time. And as you continually seek to know and follow God's purpose for your life, be patient. Your heavenly Father may not always reveal His plan as quickly or as completely as you'd like, but rest assured: God is here, and He wants to use you in wonderful, often unexpected ways. Your task is to listen, to learn, and to follow.

There's not much you can't achieve or endure if you know God is walking by your side. Just remember: Someone knows, and Someone cares.

Bill Hybels

Tapped in to God's Power

I can do everything through him who gives me strength.
Philippians 4:13 NIV

Have you really tapped in to God's power? Have you turned your life and your heart over to Him, or are you still trying to do everything by yourself?

The Bible promises that you can do great things when you avail yourself of God's power. But how can you tap in? By allowing the Creator to work in you and through you—and by placing Him squarely at the center of your heart and life.

When you accept God's love and experience His power—when you trust Him to manage His world and yours—you'll discover that He offers all the strength you need to live victoriously today, tomorrow, and forever. So don't delay. Tap in to the ultimate power source today.

When we reach the end of our strength, wisdom, and personal resources, we enter into the beginning of His glorious provisions.
Patsy Clairmont

Keeping Prosperity in Perspective

*Serving God does make us very rich, if we are satisfied
with what we have. We brought nothing into the world,
so we can take nothing out. But, if we have food
and clothes, we will be satisfied with that.*
1 Timothy 6:6–8 NCV

We live in an era of prosperity, a time when many of us have been richly blessed with an assortment of material possessions that our forebears scarcely could have imagined. Because we live in such prosperous times, we must be cautious: we must keep prosperity in perspective.

The world stresses the importance of material possessions; God stresses spiritual riches. The world promises happiness through wealth and public acclaim; God promises joy and peace that will never fade away. The difference is that only God's promises can be truly trusted.

The world often makes promises it cannot keep, but when God makes a promise, He keeps it—not just for a day or for a year or for a lifetime, but for all eternity.

*Lives based on having are less free
than lives based either on doing or on being.*
William James

First Things First

*We can't afford to waste a minute, must not squander
these precious daylight hours in frivolity and indulgence,
in sleeping around and dissipation,
in bickering and grabbing everything in sight. . . .
Dress yourselves in Christ, and be up and about!*
Romans 13:13–14 MSG

First things first." These words are easy to speak but hard to put into practice. Why? Because so many people are expecting so many things from us!

If you're having trouble prioritizing your day, perhaps you've been trying to organize your life according to your own plans, not God's. A better strategy is to take your daily obligations and place them in the hands of the One who created you. To do so, you must prioritize your day according to God's commandments, and you must seek His will and His wisdom in all matters. Then you can face the day with the assurance that the same God who created our universe out of nothingness will help you put first things first in your own life.

*You will get untold flak for prioritizing
God's revealed and present will for your life
over man's . . . but, boy, is it worth it.*
Beth Moore

Recharging Your Batteries

Come unto me, all ye that labour and are heavy laden,
and I will give you rest.
Matthew 11:28 KJV

The demands of daily life can drain us of our strength and rob us of the joy God intends for His children. When we find ourselves tired, discouraged, or worse, there is a source from which we can draw the power needed to recharge our spiritual batteries. That source is God.

God wants His children to lead joyous lives filled with spiritual abundance and peace. But sometimes those blessings can seem elusive. It is then that we must turn to God for renewal; and when we do, He will restore us.

God expects us to work hard, but He also intends for us to rest. When we fail to take the rest we need, we do a disservice to ourselves and to those around us.

Is your spiritual battery running low? Is your energy on the wane? Are your emotions frayed? If so, turn to God and accept the rest and recharging only He can offer.

Life is strenuous.
See that your clock does not run down.
Mrs. Charles E. Cowman

Speech and the Golden Rule

*A good person produces good deeds
and words season after season.*
Matthew 12:35 MSG

Matthew 7:12 instructs us, "In everything, do to others what you would have them do to you, for this sums up the Law and the Prophets" (NIV). This is God's Golden Rule. And if we are to observe the Golden Rule in everything, that includes what we say. We must be careful to speak words of encouragement, hope, and truth to all who cross our paths.

Sometimes, when we feel uplifted and secure, it's easy to speak kind words. Other times, when we're discouraged or weary or stressed, we can scarcely summon the energy to uplift ourselves, much less anyone else. But God's commandment is clear: we must observe the Golden Rule "in everything." So today, think about the words you speak and the tone in which you choose to speak them. Be sure you produce not only good deeds but good words as well.

*If you are to be self-controlled in your speech,
you must be self-controlled in your thinking.*
François Fénelon

The God Who Preserves Us

He will wipe away every tear from their eyes.
Death will exist no longer; grief, crying, and pain will exist
no longer, because the previous things have passed away.
Revelation 21:4 HCSB

People of every generation have experienced adversity, and this generation is no different. Yet it seems today we face certain challenges that previous generations didn't.

Although the world continues to change, God's love remains constant. He remains ready to comfort us and strengthen us whenever we turn to Him.

God's Word contains this promise: "The LORD is near to all who call upon Him, to all who call upon Him in truth. He will fulfill the desire of those who fear Him; He also will hear their cry and save them. The LORD preserves all who love Him" (Psalm 145:18–20 NKJV). This comforting passage reminds us that when we are troubled, we can call upon God, and in His perfect time, He will heal us. Until He does, we can take comfort in knowing that we never suffer alone . . . and that someday He will wipe every tear from our eyes.

As we focus on His love and Word,
in time He will fill our void and loneliness,
and He will heal our pain.
Anita Corrine Donihue

Focusing on God's Blessings

*Blessed is he whose help is the God of Jacob,
whose hope is in the LORD his God, the Maker of heaven
and earth, the sea, and everything in them—the LORD,
who remains faithful forever.*
Psalm 146:5–6 NIV

What is your focus today? Are you willing to center your thoughts on the countless blessings God has bestowed upon you? Before you answer that question, consider this: the direction of your thoughts will have a profound effect on the direction of your day and the quality of your life.

This day—and every day—is an opportunity to celebrate the life God has given you. It's a chance to celebrate your relationships, your talents, and your opportunities. So focus your thoughts on the gift of life and on the blessings that surround you.

You are a beautiful creation of God, loved and treasured by Him. Give thanks for your gifts, and determine to share them. Never have the needs—or the opportunities for service—been greater.

*Occupy your minds with good thoughts,
or the enemy will fill them with bad ones.
Unoccupied, they cannot be.*
Saint Thomas More

Directing Your Thoughts

Dear brothers and sisters, one final thing.
Fix your thoughts on what is true, and honorable,
and right, and pure, and lovely, and admirable.
Think about things that are excellent and worthy of praise.
Philippians 4:8 NLT

How will you direct your thoughts today? Will you obey the words of Philippians 4:8 and choose to dwell on those things that are honorable, true, and worthy of praise? Or will you allow your thoughts to be hijacked by the negativity that seems to dominate our troubled world?

Are you fearful, angry, or worried? Are you so preoccupied with the concerns of this day that you fail to thank God for the promise of eternity? Are you confused, bitter, or pessimistic? If so, it's time to redirect your thoughts to dwell on God's infinite love and His boundless grace. As you contemplate these things, and as you give thanks for God's blessings, negativity will longer dominate your day . . . or your life.

Every good thought you think is contributing
its share to the ultimate result of your life.
Grenville Kleiser

Signs

Our God forever and ever . . . will guide us until death.
Psalm 48:14 NASB

God is always present, and He is always trying to get His message through to us. If we seek to discover God's will for our lives—and we should—then we will meditate on His Word and petition Him often through heartfelt prayer. We will train ourselves to be watchful, looking for the marvelous variety of ways God answers our prayers and offers guidance. Sometimes the signs He gives us will be obvious; other times they'll be more subtle. Either way, we can discern God's will if we wait patiently with our eyes open wide and our hearts open wider.

If you're struggling to find solutions to life's toughest questions, strive to be watchful, patient, and faithful. On every step of your journey, trust your heavenly Father to show you the way: His way. Then look for the signs that He will certainly provide to guide you. When you do, you'll receive the divine insight that only God can give.

If we want to hear God's voice,
we must surrender our minds and hearts to Him.
Billy Graham

A Love That Endures

The love of the LORD remains forever with those
who fear him. His salvation extends to the children's
children of those who are faithful to his covenant,
of those who obey his commandments!
Psalm 103:17–18 NLT

The Bible contains the repeated promise that God's love endures forever. And that's a promise upon which you can rely. God's love does not depend on your status, your behavior, your thoughts, or your past. God loves you simply because you are His creation, made in His image, always close to His heart.

Have you opened your heart to your heavenly Father? Have you sincerely asked Him to rule over your day and your life? If so, God promises to bless you with His peace and His abundance.

Today and every day, take comfort in knowing that God's love endures forever. Remember that His love for you is perfect and unending. And be assured that His love is intended for you, His precious child.

Though our feelings come and go,
God's love for us does not.
C. S. Lewis

When Your Courage Is Tested

Do not fear! Stand by and see the salvation of the LORD.
Exodus 14:13 NASB

Even if you're a confident person, you may sometimes be discouraged by the disappointments and setbacks that are part and parcel of life here on earth. When times are good, it's easy to trust God; but when troubles arise, we may lose the proper perspective and, subsequently, hope. However, if we trust God's promises, we need never fear.

If your courage is being tested today, lean on God's promises. Trust the Creator of the universe to help you meet your challenges. Remember that God is always near and that He is your protector and deliverer. When you're worried, anxious, or afraid, call on Him and accept the comforting touch of His hand. God is in control, and He rules with limitless wisdom and love—now and forever.

If God has you in the palm of his hand and your real life is secure in him, then you can venture forth—into the places and relationships, the challenges, the very heart of the storm—and you will be safe there.
Paula Rinehart

When Solutions Aren't Easy

*If you don't know what you're doing, pray to the
Father. He loves to help. You'll get his help, and won't
be condescended to when you ask for it. Ask boldly,
believingly, without a second thought. People who
"worry their prayers" are like wind-whipped waves.
Don't think you're going to get anything from the Master
that way, adrift at sea, keeping all your options open.*
James 1:5–8 MSG

At one time or another in the course of our lives,
we all face problems that defy easy solutions.
If you find yourself facing a difficult decision, or a
sticky situation, here's a simple formula for making
the right choice: let God take care of it. Instead of
fretting about your future, pray about it.

When you consult your heavenly Father early and
often, you'll soon discover that the quiet moments
you spend with God can be extremely helpful. He
will quietly lead you along a path of His choosing—a
path that is right for you.

So the next time you arrive at one of life's
crossroads, take a moment or two to bow your head
and consult the Ultimate Adviser. He always knows
the best solution.

*God always gives His best
to those who leave the choice with Him.*
Jim Elliot

Speaking Words
of Encouragement and Hope

Good people's words will help many others.
Proverbs 10:21 NCV

The words we speak have the power to do great good or great harm. If we speak words of encouragement and hope, we can lift others up. And that's exactly what God wants us to do.

When the sun is shining and our hearts are at peace, it seems natural to speak kind words to family members and friends. But when the storm clouds form overhead, and when our hearts are troubled by the challenges of life, we find it more difficult to be encouraging.

God intends that we speak words of kindness, wisdom, and truth regardless of our circumstances, regardless of our emotions. That can be difficult, yet when we do speak as God desires, we share a priceless gift with the world—and we give glory to our Creator. As thoughtful, thankful men and women who seek to honor our Father in heaven, let us determine to do no less.

We do have the ability to encourage or discourage each
other with the words we say.
In order to maintain a positive mood,
our hearts must be in good condition.
Annie Chapman

Faith and Wholeness

The righteous will live by his faith.
Habakkuk 2:4 NIV

A suffering woman sought healing in an unusual way: she simply touched the hem of Jesus's garment. When she did, Jesus turned and said, "Daughter, be of good comfort; thy faith hath made thee whole" (Matthew 9:22 KJV).

We, too, can be made whole when we place our faith in the Creator of the universe. So strengthen your faith through praise, through worship, through Bible study, and through prayer. Then trust God's plans, knowing they are always for your ultimate benefit.

Jesus is standing at the door of your heart, knocking. If you open the door of your heart and invite Him in, He will give you peace and heal your broken spirit. Have faith enough to reach out to touch even the smallest fragment of the Master's garment, and He will make you whole.

Let me encourage you to continue to wait with faith.
God may not perform a miracle,
but He is trustworthy to touch you and make you whole
where there used to be a hole.
Lisa Whelchel

July

God's Faithfulness

> *The Lord is faithful; He will strengthen*
> *and guard you from the evil one.*
> 2 Thessalonians 3:3 HCSB

God is faithful to us even when we are not faithful to Him. God keeps His promises to us even when we stray far from His will. He continues to love us even when we wander off His path. God remains steadfast and ever present, always ready to bless us. Our task, simply put, is to be ready to receive His blessings.

As you prepare to meet the coming day, remember that God isn't just near, He is here—right by your side. He has promised to protect you and to guide your steps. When you open your heart to Him, He will fill it with love. When you're attentive to Him—and when you are faithful to Him—He has promised to bless you . . . and that's a promise He intends to keep.

> *The stars may fall, but God's promises*
> *will stand and be fulfilled.*
> J. I. Packer

Using Our Gifts

Based on the gift they have received,
everyone should use it to serve others,
as good managers of the varied grace of God.
1 Peter 4:10 HCSB

How do we thank God for the gifts He has given us? By using those gifts, that's how.

God has given you talents and opportunities that are uniquely yours. Are you willing to use your gifts in the way God intends? Are you willing to summon the discipline required to develop your talents and hone your skills? That's precisely what God wants you to do, and that's precisely what you should desire for yourself.

As you seek to expand your talents, you'll undoubtedly encounter stumbling blocks along the way, such as the fear of rejection or the fear of failure. When you do, don't let them throw you off the path. Just continue to refine your skills, and offer your services to God. When the time is right, He will use you—but it's up to you to be thoroughly prepared.

We must not only give what we have,
we must also give what we are.
Désiré-Joseph Mercier

God's Glorious World

God saw everything that He had made,
and indeed it was very good.
Genesis 1:31 NKJV

Each morning, the sun rises on a glorious world that's a physical manifestation of God's infinite power and His infinite love. And yet we're sometimes too busy to notice.

We live in a society filled with more distractions than we can possibly count and more obligations than we can possibly meet. Is it any wonder, then, that we often overlook God's handiwork as we rush from place to place, giving scarcely a single thought to the beauty that surrounds us?

Today, take time to really observe the world around you. Take time to offer a prayer of thanks for the sky above and for all the beauty that lies beneath it. Ponder the miracle of God's creation. The time you spend celebrating God's wonderful world is always time well spent.

No philosophical theory which I have yet come across is a
radical improvement on the words
of Genesis, that "in the beginning
God made Heaven and Earth."
C. S. Lewis

God's Watchful Eye

O Lord, you have examined my heart and know everything
about me. You know when I sit down or stand up.
You know my thoughts even when I'm far away. . . .
You know everything I do.
Psalm 139:1–3 NLT

God is all-knowing. Even when nobody else is watching, God is watching. Even when we believe that our actions (and their consequences) will be known only to ourselves, our Creator sees our every deed. God knows that we're not perfect, and He understands that we will make mistakes; but He wants us to live according to His rules, not our own. And when we refuse, He is not obligated to protect us from the natural consequences of our mistakes or rebellious acts.

The next time you're tempted to say something you shouldn't say or do, remember that you can't keep secrets from God. But when you live according to His guidelines, you open yourself up to the blessings He so generously gives to those who follow Him.

God possesses infinite knowledge and awareness
which is [sic] uniquely His. At all times, even in the midst
of any type of suffering, I can realize that He knows, loves,
watches, understands, and more than that, He has a purpose.
Billy Graham

Your Spiritual Journey

*Dear brothers and sisters, when troubles come your way,
consider it an opportunity for great joy.
For you know that when your faith is tested,
your endurance has a chance to grow.*
James 1:2–3 NLT

The journey toward spiritual maturity lasts a lifetime. This truth was not lost on Norman Vincent Peale, who offered the following advice: "Ask the God who made you to keep remaking you." Sound advice . . . but how often do we take it?

When we cease to grow, either emotionally or spiritually, we do ourselves a profound disservice. But if we study God's Word, if we obey His commandments, if we trust His promises, and if we live in the center of His will, we won't become stagnant. Instead, we'll keep growing . . . and that's exactly what God wants for us.

Are you "fully grown"? If you're honest, you'll admit that you're not—and that, in truth, you never will be in this life. On your spiritual journey, there's always room for growth.

*The Holy Spirit was given to guide us into all truth, but
He doesn't do it all at once.*
Elisabeth Elliot

Time for Silence

Be silent before Me.
Isaiah 41:1 HCSB

One good way to know God is to be still and listen to Him. But sometimes you may find it hard to slow down and listen. As the many demands and distractions of everyday life call out to you, it's easy to become so wrapped up in your obligations that you just don't take enough time out to spend communing with God.

But if you'll make the time and the effort to quiet yourself each day and listen for the Father's voice, you'll be rewarded: you'll experience His presence and be enveloped in His love. If you will wait for Him, God will touch your heart; He will restore your spirit; and He will give you the perspective you need to make good decisions about all those other things clamoring for your attention. So why not go to Him right now? If you really want to know your heavenly Father, silence is a wonderful place to start.

The world is full of noise. Might we not set ourselves to learn silence, stillness, solitude?
Elisabeth Elliot

Life Triumphant

Shout triumphantly to the LORD, all the earth.
Serve the LORD with gladness;
come before Him with joyful songs.
Psalm 100:1–2 HCSB

Are you living the triumphant life that God has promised can be yours? Or are you a spiritual shrinking violet? As you ponder that question, consider this: God does not intend for you to live a life that is merely mediocre. And He doesn't want you to hide the light He has placed within you. He wants you to "Let your light so shine before men, that they may see your good works and glorify your Father in heaven" (Matthew 5:16 NKJV). In short, your heavenly Father wants you to live a triumphant life so that others might know what it means to be a child of God.

Life should be a triumphal celebration, a daily exercise in thanksgiving and praise. Join that celebration today . . . and live so that you and others can see God's light and join the celebration, too.

The great thing is to be found at one's post as a child
of God, living each day as though it were our last, but
planning as though our world might last a hundred years.
C. S. Lewis

Checking Your Balance

*No servant can serve two masters. The servant will
hate one master and love the other, or will follow
one master and refuse to follow the other.
You cannot serve both God and worldly riches.*
Luke 16:13 NCV

Your money can be used to bless your loved ones
and others, and it can even be a blessing to
yourself. But beware: in our society, it's all too easy
to place far too much emphasis on money and the
things money can buy. We must not lose sight of the
fact that God cares about people, not possessions—
and so must we.

Money, in and of itself, is not evil; but
worshipping money—putting it before God and those
He has called us to love and serve—is wrong. When
we worship God, we'll be blessed. But if we worship
"the almighty dollar," we'll inevitably pay a price for
our misplaced priorities.

So today, check your balance of spiritual and
financial matters. As you prioritize matters of
importance, make sure you're not serving money but
rather using your money to serve God.

Money is a terrible master but an excellent servant.
P. T. Barnum

The Power of Perspective

Teach me Your way, O LORD; I will walk in Your truth.
Psalm 86;11 NASB

For most of us, life is busy and complicated. Amid the rush and crush of the daily grind, it's easy to lose perspective. But we must not let that happen. When our world seems to be spinning out of control, we must seek to regain a proper perspective by slowing down and turning our thoughts and prayers toward God.

Each morning, as we awaken to a new day—and to a new set of challenges—the pressures of everyday life can overtake our thoughts and our hearts *if* we let them. That's why we should consult the Creator early and often. When we do, He will touch our hearts; He will calm our fears; He will lift our spirits; and He will help us keep our challenges in perspective.

Would you like a daily dose of proper perspective? Then ask God. He will answer and help you to walk in His truth.

The proper perspective creates within us
a spirit of reaching outside of ourselves
with joy and enthusiasm.
Luci Swindoll

The Power of Prayer

If you believe, you will receive
whatever you ask for in prayer.
Matthew 21:22 HCSB

"The power of prayer": these words are so familiar that sometimes we forget what they mean. Prayer is a powerful tool for communicating with our Creator; it's an opportunity to interact with the Giver of life. And prayer improves our lives, helping us find strength for today and hope for the future. Prayer is not a thing to be taken lightly—or to be used infrequently.

Is prayer an integral part of your daily life, or is it more hit-or-miss than habit? Do you "pray without ceasing," or is prayer something you do only when you've tried everything else—an afterthought?

Prayer changes things . . . and it changes us. So today, instead of worrying about your next decision, ask God to lead the way. Pray constantly about things great and small. God is listening; He wants to hear from you; and He has promised to answer.

I have been driven many times to my knees by
the overwhelming conviction that I had nowhere else to go.
My own wisdom, and that of all
about me, seemed insufficient for the day.
Abraham Lincoln

God's Big Plans for You

It is better to take refuge in the LORD
than to trust in man.
Psalm 118:8 HCSB

Does God have big plans for your life? Of course He does! Every day of your life, He is speaking, wanting to lead you along a path of His choosing . . . but He won't force you to follow. The Creator has given you free will: the ability and opportunity to make decisions for yourself. The choices are yours, so the consequences—including rewards when you choose wisely—are yours as well.

Today, as you spend time with your heavenly Father, ask Him to renew your sense of purpose. God's plans for you may be far bigger and better than you imagine, but He may be waiting for you to make the next move. So make that move prayerfully, faithfully, and expectantly. And then trust God to make His.

Yesterday is just experience, but tomorrow is glistening
with purpose—and today is the channel
leading from one to the other.
Barbara Johnson

The Value of Self-Discipline

Discipline yourself for the purpose of godliness.
1 Timothy 4:7 NASB

God's Word instructs us to lead lives of discipline, diligence, moderation, and maturity. But the world often tempts us to do otherwise. Everywhere we turn, it seems, we're faced with powerful temptations to behave in undisciplined or ungodly ways. But our Creator has far better plans for our days and for our lives.

In order to see those plans realized, we must do our part by being disciplined in our thoughts and our actions. The Bible warns against the dangers of impulsive behavior; it teaches us that diligence is rewarded, but laziness will bring harm in the long run.

Do you wish to reap the rewards God offers those who lead disciplined lives? If so, determine to discipline yourself today so that God can accomplish His purpose in and through you.

The feeling of being valuable is a cornerstone of self-discipline because when one considers oneself valuable, one will care for oneself in all ways that are necessary. Self-discipline is self-caring.
M. Scott Peck

Real Treasures

> *Collect for yourselves treasures in heaven,*
> *where neither moth nor rust destroys, and where thieves*
> *don't break in and steal. For where your treasure is,*
> *there your heart will be also.*
> Matthew 6:20–21 HCSB

The world encourages us to treasure material possessions, but God has other intentions. His Word instructs us to gather spiritual treasures, not physical ones. And His Word promises that we will be blessed when we do.

In the sixth chapter of Matthew, Jesus teaches us to trust God for the things we need and to focus our energies not on accumulating material wealth but on serving the Creator. It's a lesson we must never forget, especially amid the general prosperity of life here in the twenty-first century.

Society teaches us to honor possessions, but God teaches us to honor Him, and that's good—because earthly treasures are here today and all too soon gone. Our real riches, of course, are in heaven (thank goodness!), and that's where we should direct our thoughts, our energies, and our prayers.

We own too many things that aren't worth owning.
Marie T. Freeman

Always Thanksgiving

Our prayers for you are always spilling over into thanksgivings. We can't quit thanking God our Father and Jesus our Messiah for you!
Colossians 1:3 MSG

Sometimes life can be complicated, demanding, and frustrating. When the push and pull of living leaves us rushing from place to place with barely a moment to spare, we can forget to pause and thank our Creator for the countless blessings He bestows upon us. Giving thanks brings our focus back onto the many blessings God has placed in our lives. And when we truly appreciate the things and people He has sent our way, our hearts will overflow with even more thanksgiving. But when we look past our blessings and focus on our problems or even just our obligations, we forfeit the joy that comes with a thankful heart.

Don't cheat yourself. As a person who has been promised and given much by your heavenly Father, determine to make thanksgiving a habit, beginning today.

Thanksgiving or complaining—these words express two contrastive attitudes of the souls of God's children in regard to His dealings with them. The soul that gives thanks can find comfort in everything; the soul that complains can find comfort in nothing.
Hannah Whitall Smith

Being Understood

*Dear friends, if God loved us in this way,
we also must love one another.*
1 John 4:11 HCSB

What a blessing it is when our friends and loved ones genuinely seek to understand who we are and what we think. And just as we seek to be understood by others, so we should seek to understand the hopes and dreams of our family members and friends.

We live in a busy world, a place where it's easy to overlook the needs of others. But God knows every need and understands every heart. He loves each person, and He has called us to love one another. So today, honor God by showing love to His children. Slow down long enough to notice the trials and tribulations of those around you, and give the gift of understanding not just to friends and family members but to those who are different from you or even to someone you've just met. It may take a little extra effort, but you never know what treasures of friendship may be just waiting to be discovered.

*Don't bypass the potential for meaningful friendships just
because of differences.
Explore them. Embrace them. Love them.*
Luci Swindoll

The Rewards of Work

The plans of the diligent lead surely to plenty.
Proverbs 21:5 NKJV

How does God intend for us to work? Does He intend for us to work diligently, or does He reward mediocrity? The answer should be obvious. God has created a world in which hard work is rewarded and sloppy work is not. Yet sometimes we may seek ease over excellence, or we may be tempted to take shortcuts when God wants us to walk the straight and narrow path.

Today, heed God's Word by doing good work. Wherever you find yourself, whatever your job description, do your work, and do it with all your heart. When you do, you'll likely win the recognition of your peers. But more importantly, God will bless your efforts and use you in ways that only He can foresee. So work faithfully . . . and leave the rest to God.

I am more and more persuaded
that all that is required of us is faithful seed-sowing.
The harvest is bound to follow.
Annie Armstrong

Taking Your Worries to God

Give your worries to the LORD, and he will take care
of you. He will never let good people down.
Psalm 55:22 NCV

Because life is sometimes difficult, and because we understandably have fears about an uncertain future, we worry. At times we may fret over the countless details involved in the business of living. We may worry about our relationships, our finances, our health, or any number of potential problems, some large and some small.

If you're a worrier by nature, begin this new day by rethinking the way you think. Perhaps you've formed the unfortunate habit of focusing too intently on the negative aspects of life while spending too little time counting your blessings. If so, take your worries to God . . . and leave them with Him. Trust Him to take care of you. When you do, your burdens will be lighter and your future brighter. God is looking out for you—you can trust Him with your life, because He has promised never to let you down.

Today is the tomorrow we worried about yesterday.
Dennis Swanberg

Expecting God's Blessings

My cup runs over. Surely goodness and mercy
shall follow me all the days of my life;
and I will dwell in the house of the LORD forever.
Psalm 23:5–6 NKJV

As you look at the landscape of your life, do you see opportunities, possibilities, and blessings, or do you focus on gloomier aspects of the scenery? Do you look forward and anticipate blessings or misfortunes? If you've been focusing more on the clouds than the silver lining, perhaps your spiritual vision is in need of correction.

Today is a glorious gift from God, and it presents a golden opportunity to thank Him for His gifts and to express faith in His continued goodness.

The way you choose to view the world around you will have a profound impact on the quality, the tone, and the direction of your life. The more you focus on the beauty that surrounds you and look forward to God's promised blessings, the more beautiful your own life will become.

Every day we live is a priceless gift of God,
loaded with possibilities to learn something new,
to gain fresh insights.
Dale Evans Rogers

God's Healing Touch

"I will give peace, real peace, to those far and near,
and I will heal them," says the LORD.
Isaiah 57:19 NCV

Are you concerned about your spiritual, physical, or emotional health? If so, you'll find a timeless source of comfort, assurance, and healing that's as near as your next breath. That source is God.

Your heavenly Father is concerned about every aspect of your life, including your health. And when you face concerns about any aspect of your well-being, including health-related challenges, God is with you. So trust your medical doctor to do his or her part, and turn to your family and friends for moral, physical, and spiritual support. But be sure to place your ultimate trust in your benevolent and powerful Creator. Only He has the power to heal you, body, mind, and soul.

If you want to receive emotional healing from God and
come into an area of wholeness, you must realize that
healing is a process, and you must allow the Lord to deal
with you and your problem in
His own way and in His own time.
Joyce Meyer

Your Abundant Harvest

When you're joined with me and I with you,
the relation intimate and organic,
the harvest is sure to be abundant.
John 15:5 MSG

The Bible offers hope—God's Word promises that when we open our hearts to Him, we will experience abundance and peace. As you face the rigors of everyday life, will you take God at His Word? If you will, you can expect Him to shower you with blessings now and throughout eternity.

In every circumstance of life, during times of wealth or times of want, God has promised to provide precisely what you need if you'll trust Him (see Matthew 6). So trust your heavenly Father to provide for your spiritual, emotional, and material needs. When you turn these concerns over to Him, you can be sure He will fulfill His promises.

God can manage every situation, and He can give you the spiritual abundance you so earnestly desire.

People, places, and things
were never meant to give us life.
God alone is the author of a fulfilling life.
Gary Smalley

Avoiding Foolish Arguments

*Stay away from those who have foolish arguments
and talk about useless family histories and argue
and quarrel about the law. Those things are worth
nothing and will not help anyone.*

Titus 3:9 NCV

Arguments are seldom won but often lost. When we engage in petty squabbles, our losses usually outweigh our gains. And if we allow ourselves to fall into habitual bickering, we'll do harm to our friends, to our families, to our coworkers, and to ourselves.

Time and again, God's Word teaches us that most arguments are a monumental waste of time, of energy, of life. In the book of Titus we are warned to refrain from "foolish arguments," and with good reason. Such arguments are usually frustrating, infuriating, and futile. So the next time you're tempted to engage in a foolish feud, refrain. When you do, you'll put a smile on God's face, and you'll send the devil packing.

*You don't have to attend every argument
you're invited to.*

Source unknown

On a Mission

God made everything with a place and purpose.
Proverbs 16:4 MSG

Whether you realize it or not, you are on a personal mission for God: to honor Him, to follow His instructions, and to serve His children.

You will encounter impediments as you attempt to discover the exact nature of God's purpose for your life, but you must never lose sight of the overriding purposes that God has established for all of us. You will be reminded of these purposes again and again as you worship your Creator and study His Word.

Each day is a new opportunity to live out your mission to serve God and to worship Him. When you do so, He will bless you in miraculous ways. May you continue to seek God's will; may you trust His promises; and may you find your place and fulfill His purpose for your life and in the world.

Whatever purpose motivates your life,
it must be something big enough and grand enough to
make the investment worthwhile.
Warren Wiersbe

Choosing to Walk in His Footsteps

*Walk in a manner worthy of the God who calls you into
His own kingdom and glory.*
1 Thessalonians 2:12 NASB

Because we are creatures of free will, we make choices—lots of them. When we make choices that are pleasing to our heavenly Father, we will be blessed by Him. When we choose to follow in the footsteps of God's Son, we will enjoy the abundance God has promised to those who follow Jesus.

Unfortunately, sometimes we make choices that are displeasing to God. We sow seeds that have the potential to bring an unhappy harvest.

Today, as you go about what seems like the routine of daily living, you will actually be making hundreds of choices. Will you choose wisely? Start by making your thoughts and your actions pleasing to your Creator. Then make every choice as if God were watching . . . because He is.

It is always your next move.
Napoleon Hill

Hospitality

Be hospitable to one another without grumbling.
1 Peter 4:9 NKJV

Did Jesus instruct us in matters of courtesy and hospitality? You may be surprised to learn that He did. In fact, His instructions are clear: "In everything, therefore, treat people the same way you want them to treat you" (Matthew 7:12 NASB). Jesus did not say, "In some things, treat people as you wish to be treated." And He did not say, "From time to time, be friendly and welcoming." Jesus said that we should treat others as we wish to be treated—in every aspect of our daily lives. This is a tall order indeed, but we must to do our best.

Today, show a little extra hospitality to those you meet, always remembering the ultimate hospitality God has shown toward you by calling you friend and welcoming you into His family and His eternal home. Show your gratitude to Him by the way you interact with others.

Reach out and care for someone who needs
the touch of hospitality. The time you spend caring today
will be a love gift that will blossom into
the fresh joy of God's Spirit in the future.
Emilie Barnes

Great Expectations

A dream fulfilled is a tree of life.
Proverbs 13:12 NLT

Do you expect your future to be bright? Are you willing to dream king-size dreams . . . and are you willing to work diligently to make those dreams come true?

The apostle Paul said, "I can do all things through Christ who strengthens me" (Philippians 4:13 NKJV). Yet most of us, even the most faithful among us, often live far below our potential. We take half measures; we dream small dreams; we waste precious time and energy on the distractions of the world. But God has better plans for us.

Our Creator intends that we live faithfully, hopefully, courageously, and abundantly. He knows that with His help we are capable of great things, and He has great expectations. Do you?

If you pour your heart into your work,
or any other enterprise, you can achieve dreams others may
think impossible.
Howard Schultz

Perseverance Pays

Don't try to get out of anything prematurely.
Let it do its work so you become mature
and well-developed, not deficient in any way.
James 1:4 MSG

He lived in an age when poetry was considered a young man's game, but he was almost forty years old and had never published a single book of poems. Still, Robert Frost didn't give up. Instead, he sold his farm and became a full-time poet.

Persistence paid off for Frost, who became the most noted poet of his time. And what worked for Frost will work for you, too. Perseverance pays.

Are you facing a difficult challenge, and have you been tempted to call it quits? If so, it's time to remind yourself that life's greatest rewards usually accrue to those who work hard—and keep working hard. So don't give up, because as Robert Frost demonstrated, persistent people prevail . . . it's simply poetic justice.

Just don't give up trying to do what you really
want to do. Where there's love and inspiration,
I don't think you can go wrong.
Ella Fitzgerald

Giving Your Best Performance

May the Lord our God show us his approval
and make our efforts successful.
Yes, make our efforts successful!
Psalm 90:17 NLT

Just six years after graduating from the University of North Carolina, a young actor starred on Broadway in the play *No Time for Sergeants*. Then, in 1960, he starred in a show that bore his name: *The Andy Griffith Show*. Griffith portrayed Sheriff Andy Taylor, an insightful public servant with a heart of gold—and in real life, Griffith wasn't very different from his TV character.

Griffith offered this advice for life: "Approach everything realistically, and give it the best caring effort you know how." That's a recipe for success that would make the citizens of Mayberry proud . . . and one that you'll find effective in whatever town you live.

So take it from Andy: get up on life's stage and give your performance everything you've got. When you give it your all and trust God to make your efforts successful, He'll give your story a happy ending.

The best performance is yet to be.
Maurice Chevalier

The Gift of Generosity

God will generously provide all you need.
Then you will always have everything you need
and plenty left over to share with others.
2 Corinthians 9:8 NLT

In 2 Corinthians 9:8, you'll find an important promise, and one upon which you can depend. The Creator of the universe has promised to provide for all your needs. In fact, He will not only meet your needs; He will generously give you more than you need to survive. But notice the last part of the verse: God provides for you generously so that you can share the surplus with others. He blesses you so that you can be a blessing to those He places along your path.

Are you worried about your material needs? Don't be—God will give you what you need. But once you have enough to meet your requirements, He asks you to share with others. When you do, you'll be a partner in God's work in the world, and He will bless you—not just for today, but for every day of your life.

We shall find in Christ enough of everything
we need—for the body, for the mind,
and for the spirit—to do what He wants us to do
as long as He wants us to do it.
Vance Havner

Our Refuge

God is our refuge and strength,
a very present help in trouble.
Psalm 46:1 NKJV

We live in a world that can be, at times, a frightening place. It can be a discouraging place. It's a world in which losses can be so painful and profound that they change our lives, and it seems we'll never get over them. But with God's help, and with the help of encouraging family members and friends, we can recover.

During the darker days of life, we'll be wise to remember that God is with us always and that He offers us comfort, assurance, and peace—we must simply turn to Him as our refuge and look to Him for strength and help.

When we trust in God and in His promises, the world becomes a less frightening place. With God's comfort and His love in our hearts, we can tackle our problems with courage, determination, and faith.

Put your hand into the hand of God.
He gives the calmness and serenity
of heart and soul.
Mrs. Charles E. Cowman

Compassionate Neighbors

If you really carry out the royal law prescribed in Scripture,
You shall love your neighbor as yourself,
you are doing well.
James 2:8 HCSB

The Bible instructs us to be compassionate neighbors—and God's Word promises that when we follow these instructions, we will be blessed. But sometimes we fall short. Sometimes, amid the busyness and confusion of everyday life, we may neglect to share a kind word or a kind deed. This oversight hurts others, and it hurts us as well.

Today, be a compassionate neighbor. Slow down and be alert for friends who need your smile, your kind words, or your helping hand. Make kindness a centerpiece of your dealings with others. They will be blessed, and you will be, too.

It's always the right time to honor God by caring for His children. Do this, and you'll be doing well.

Seek to do good, and you will find
that happiness will run after you.
James Freeman Clarke

Relying on God's Promises

Sustain me as You promised, and I will live;
do not let me be ashamed of my hope.
Psalm 119:116 HCSB

God has made many promises to you, and He will keep every single one of them. You can trust God's Word in every situation you will ever encounter. No exceptions.

Are you facing a difficult decision? Pause for a moment and have a quiet consultation with your Adviser. Are you fearful, fretful, or troubled? Slow down long enough to meditate on God's promises. Are you going through a difficult time in your life? Ask God to help you—after all, that's precisely what He's promised to do.

God's promises never fail, and they never grow old. You can rely upon those promises. And you do well to share the hope you've found in God with your family, with your friends, and with the world . . . so they can know and rely on God's promises, too.

Only God knows when everything in and around is fully
ripe for the manifestation of the blessings
that have been given to faith. . . .
It is through faith and patience
we inherit the promises.
Andrew Murray

August

God's Sufficiency

My grace is sufficient for you,
for My strength is made perfect in weakness.
2 Corinthians 12:9 NKJV

Of this you can be sure: God is sufficient to meet your needs. Whatever dangers you may face, whatever heartbreaks you must endure, God is with you, and He stands ready to comfort you and to heal you. In times of intense sadness, we can turn to Him, and we should encourage our friends and family members to do likewise.

If you are experiencing the deep pain of a recent loss, or if you're still mourning a loss from long ago, perhaps you're ready to begin the next stage of your journey with God. If so, be mindful of this truth: the loving heart of God is sufficient to meet any challenge, including yours. Trust Him today, and you'll find that His grace is sufficient.

Why rely on yourself and fall?
Cast yourself upon His arm.
Be not afraid. He will not let you slip.
Saint Augustine

The Self-Fulfilling Prophecy

I will hope continually,
and will praise You yet more and more.
Psalm 71:14 NASB

The self-fulfilling prophecy is alive, well, and living at your house. If you trust God and have faith for the future, your optimistic beliefs will help give you direction and motivation. That's one reason you should never lose hope, but certainly not the only reason. The primary reason you should never lose hope is because of God's unfailing promises.

Make no mistake about it: thoughts are powerful things. Your thoughts can lift you up or pull you down. When you acquire the habit of hopeful thinking, you will have acquired a powerful tool for improving your life. So next time you find yourself falling into negative thinking, think again. Put your hope in God and offer praise to Him, and you'll find your days looking brighter.

The choice for me is to either look at all things
I have lost or the things I have. To live in fear
or to live in hope. Hope comes from knowing
I have a sovereign, loving God
who is in every event in my life.
Lisa Beamer

Choose Kindness

God has chosen you and made you his holy people.
He loves you. So always do these things: Show mercy
to others, be kind, humble, gentle, and patient.
Colossians 3:12 NCV

Kindness is a choice. We can either choose to behave kindly toward others—and by doing so reap the rich rewards God has promised for those who obey His Word—or we can allow the frustrations of everyday life to contaminate our hearts and our friendships. This choice, the decision to be kind (whether we feel actually feel like being kind or not), affects the quality, the quantity, and the duration of our relationships.

Today, even if you're feeling tired or rushed or frustrated, make the decision to spread kindness wherever you go. Be quick to smile, quick to encourage, and quick to offer a heartfelt hug. When you do, you'll discover that kindness is contagious— and that's good, because this old world needs all the kindness it can get, and so do your friends. And so, for that matter, do you.

Kindness is the universal language
that all people understand.
Jake Gaither

Believing in Miracles

With God's power working in us,
God can do much, much more than anything
we can ask or imagine.
Ephesians 3:20 NCV

Do you believe in an all-powerful God who can do miraculous things in you and through you? You should. But perhaps, as you've faced the struggles of life, you have—without realizing it—allowed them to erode your faith in a miracle-working God. If so, take the opportunity today to refresh your faith. Remember that God's power has no limitations, and be assured that He can work mighty miracles in your life.

Do you lack a firm faith in God's power to perform miracles for you and your loved ones? Spend time meditating on His promises. Read some of the stories recorded in the Bible of how God has worked miracles throughout history. Then, instead of doubting your heavenly Father, place yourself in His hands. Instead of questioning God's power, trust it. Expect Him to work miracles, because He can do even more than you could ever ask or imagine.

Live from miracle to miracle.
Artur Rubinstein

Showing Gratitude

Since we receive a kingdom which cannot be shaken,
let us show gratitude, by which we may offer to God
an acceptable service with reverence and awe.
Hebrews 12:28 NASB

For most of us, life is busy and complicated. We have countless responsibilities, some of which begin before sunrise and many of which end long after sunset. Amid the rush and crush of the daily grind, it's easy to lose sight of our blessings. But when we forget to slow down and say thank you for the gifts we've been given, we rob ourselves of opportunities to show gratitude to God for the blessings He has bestowed on us.

We can either rush through the day with scarcely a word of thanksgiving, or we can slow down and give thanks. Kahlil Gibran had this simple advice: "Wake at dawn with a winged heart and give thanks for another day of loving." When we follow that advice, gratitude will bring its own reward . . . but not its only reward.

No duty is more urgent than
that of returning thanks.
Saint Ambrose

Good Pressures, Bad Pressures

Do not be fooled:
"Bad friends will ruin good habits."
1 Corinthians 15:33 NCV

Our world is filled with pressures: some good, some bad. The pressures that we feel to behave responsibly are positive pressures. God places these pressures on our hearts and in our lives to help guide us to live rightly and well. But we also feel different pressures, ones that definitely are not from God.

Society seeks to mold us into more worldly beings. God seeks to mold us into new beings, more spiritual beings—beings that are decidedly not conformed to the world.

If we desire to lead responsible lives—and if we seek to please God—we must resist the pressures to pull away from God and His ways. We must resist the temptation to do the popular thing and insist, instead, on doing the right thing.

Those who follow the crowd
usually get lost in it.
Rick Warren

Your Potential

*Have faith in the LORD your God,
and you will stand strong.
Have faith in his prophets, and you will succeed.*
2 Chronicles 20:20 NCV

Your life is brimming with potential. God has placed you in a particular location, with specific skills, and with unique opportunities to grow and to serve. Your challenge, of course, is to make the most of these opportunities while you can.

Reaching your full potential is never easy. It takes work, and lots of it, to transform raw talent into a polished skill. But with God's help, you can do it.

In her diary, Anne Frank wrote, "The good news is that you really don't know how great you can be, how much you can love, what you can accomplish, and what your potential is." These words apply to you. You possess great potential, potential that you must use or forfeit. And the time to fulfill that potential is now.

*If I were to wish for anything, I should not wish for wealth
and power, but for the passionate sense
of the potential, for the eye which,
ever young and ardent, sees the possible.*
Søren Kierkegaard

Problem-Solving 101

Teach me to do Your will, for You are my God.
May Your gracious Spirit lead me on level ground.
Psalm 143:10 HCSB

Life is an exercise in problem solving. The question is not whether we will encounter problems; the real question is how we will choose to address them. When it comes to solving the problems of everyday living, we often know precisely what needs to be done, but we may be slow in doing it—especially if what needs to be done is difficult or uncomfortable for us. So we put off till tomorrow what should be done today.

God promises that He will help solve problems for "people who do what is right" (Psalm 34:19 NCV). And sometimes doing "what is right" means doing the uncomfortable work of confronting our problems sooner rather than later. So today, ask God to help you solve your problems. His gracious Spirit will lead you.

Always remember that problems contain values
that have improvement potential.
Norman Vincent Peale

Right with God

*The Good News shows how God makes people right
with himself—that it begins and ends with faith.
As the Scripture says, "But those who are right
with God will live by trusting in him."*
Romans 1:17 NCV

How do we live a life that is "right with God"? By trusting His promises, by obeying His commandments, and by following in the footsteps of His Son. Following in Jesus's footsteps means choosing carefully and wisely as you encounter hundreds of decisions each day. In each situation, what would Jesus do?

Whose steps will you follow today? Will you honor God by following His Son? Or will you join the lockstep legion that seeks temporary happiness and fulfillment through worldly means?

Today, follow Jesus. Strive every day to walk in His footsteps without reservation or doubt. When you live this life of faith, you'll be "right with God" . . . and that's the best way to live.

*The God we seek is a God who is intrinsically righteous
and who will be so forever.
With His example and His strength,
we can share in that righteousness.*
Bill Hybels

Opportunities for Service

Let us try to do what makes peace and helps one another.
Romans 14:19 NCV

You're a special person, created by God, and He has unique work for you to do. Do you value the unique way your heavenly Father has made you and celebrate the one-of-a-kind opportunities He has placed before you?

Too many of us have fallen into a trap—the trap of taking ourselves, our gifts, and our opportunities for granted. But God has given us the gifts and opportunities we have for a reason—so that we'll use them as He leads us.

God created you with an amazing array of talents, and He placed you precisely where you are—at a time of His choosing. God has done His part by giving you life, love, blessings, and opportunities. Your situation is unique, and so are your opportunities for service. Today, determine to use what God has given you to help others and, in so doing, to bring Him glory . . . and to bring the blessing of peace to you and to others.

Service is the pathway to real significance.
Rick Warren

What We Become

Every good gift and every perfect gift is from above,
and cometh down from the Father of lights.
James 1:17 KJV

The old saying is both familiar and true: "What we are is God's gift to us; what we become is our gift to God." Each of us possesses special talents, given to us by God, that can be nurtured or neglected. Our challenge is to use our abilities to the greatest extent possible and to use them in ways that honor our Creator.

Are you using your gifts, your God-given talents, to make the world a better place? If so, congratulations. But if you have some gifts that you haven't fully explored and developed, have a little chat with the One who gave you those gifts in the first place. Ask Him how He wants you to use those gifts, and ask Him to help you do just that. Your talents are priceless treasures from your heavenly Father. Don't let them go to waste.

With ordinary talent and extraordinary perseverance, all
things are attainable.
Thomas Buxton

The Poison of Pessimism

We are hoping for something we do not have yet,
and we are waiting for it patiently.
Romans 8:25 NCV

Pessimism is intellectual poison. Negativity can harm your heart and impair your life if you let it. So if you've allowed negative thoughts to creep into your mind, here's your assignment: start spending more time thinking about your blessings and meditating on the promises in God's Word. Train yourself to hope in Him and to look forward to all the wonderful ways His promises will be fulfilled in your life.

This day, in fact every day, is a gift from God, and He has filled it to the brim with possibilities. But persistent pessimism can rob you of the energy you need to accomplish the most important tasks on your to-do list. So today, be careful to direct your thoughts toward positive things. Refuse to swallow the poison of pessimism; instead, drink in all the goodness God has to offer. Then, wait patiently for the blessings God has promised to those who hope in Him.

Great teachers down through the ages have described the
importance of our mind
and of being master over our thoughts.
John M. Templeton

Overcoming the World

Whatever has been born of God conquers the world.
This is the victory that has conquered the world: our faith.
1 John 5:4 HCSB

All of us face times of adversity. On occasion, we all must endure the disappointments and tragedies that befall us as fragile human beings. Yet the reassuring words of 1 John 5:4 remind us that when we accept God's grace, we go from being victims to being victorious. God will enable us to overcome the temporary hardships of this world when we rely on His strength, His love, and His promise of eternal life.

When we face the inevitable difficulties of life, God stands ready to deliver us. When we call upon Him in heartfelt prayer, He will answer—in His own time and according to His own plan—and He will heal us. And while we're waiting for God's plans to unfold and for His healing touch to restore us, we can be comforted in the knowledge that our Creator can surmount any obstacle. Through faith in Him, we can be true overcomers.

Faith is the victory! Faith is the victory!
Oh, glorious victory, that overcomes the world.
John H. Yates

How to Be Holy

*Be holy in everything you do, just as God
who chose you is holy. For the Scriptures say,
"You must be holy because I am holy."*
1 Peter 1:15–16 NLT

The Bible teaches us to honor God by obeying His commandments. And it assures us that when we honor our heavenly Father, He takes notice of our actions and will bless us beyond measure.

When we live in obedience to God—which is what being holy means—and when we seek the companionship of those who do likewise, we'll reap the spiritual rewards that God truly desires us to enjoy. When we strive to do what's right, He blesses us in more ways than we can even anticipate.

So today, as you go about your many responsibilities, hold fast to that which is good. Associate with men and women who are doing their best to follow God. When you do, your right living will serve as a powerful example for others and as a worthy offering to your Creator.

*Study the Bible and observe how the persons behaved and
how God dealt with them.
There is explicit teaching on every condition of life.*
Corrie ten Boom

Managing Change

The wise see danger ahead and avoid it,
but fools keep going and get into trouble.
Proverbs 27:12 NCV

Our world is changing constantly, it seems. How will you manage all those changes? Will you do your best and trust God with the rest, or will you spend fruitless hours worrying about things you can't control? How you answer these questions is an indicator of the level of your wisdom.

If you look ahead and make plans to handle what you see coming your way, you can avoid much of the danger inherent in living by managing change with your eyes and heart open . . . and with God by your side. The same God who created the universe will guide you and protect you if you ask Him. So today, be sure to ask Him—not just for protection but for wisdom to know how to handle all the changes life throws at you. Determine to trust and serve God, for only He never changes.

When I am secure in Christ, I can afford
to take a risk in my life. Only the insecure cannot
afford to risk failure. The secure can be honest about
themselves; they can admit failure; they are able to seek
help and try again. They can change.
John Maxwell

A Clean Conscience

Let us come near to God with a sincere heart
and a sure faith, because we have been made free
from a guilty conscience,
and our bodies have been washed with pure water.
Hebrews 10:22 NCV

It has been said that character is what we are when nobody's watching. And it's true. We've all known of people (maybe they've even been us at one time or another) who, when they do things they know aren't right, try to hide their deeds from their families and friends. But even if no one else sees, God is watching.

Few things in life torment us more than a guilty conscience. And few things in life provide more contentment than the knowledge that we are obeying the conscience God has placed in our hearts.

If you want to create the best possible life for yourself and your loved ones, strive to keep a clear conscience by tuning in to God and obeying His commands. When you walk with God, your character will fall into step, too . . . and you won't need to look over your shoulder to see who, besides God, is watching.

A quiet conscience sleeps in thunder.
Thomas Fuller

Dealing with Difficult People

Bad temper is contagious—don't get infected.
Proverbs 22:25 MSG

We all know that people can be difficult to deal with . . . sometimes extremely difficult. When others are unkind to you, you may be tempted to strike back—either verbally or in some other way. But resist that temptation. Instead, remember that God will deal with those people's behavior in His own way. Even though sometimes you'll want to volunteer, He doesn't need your help.

When other people behave cruelly, foolishly, or impulsively—as they will from time to time—it's easy to let their attitudes infect us. But keep your temper in check, and don't respond in kind. Instead, speak up for yourself as politely as you can, and walk away. Let it go. Do your best to forgive everybody as quickly as you can, and leave the rest up to God.

*Bear with the faults of others as you would have them
bear with yours.*
Phillips Brooks

When We're Weak

*He told me, ". . . My strength comes into its own
in your weakness." Once I heard that, I was glad to let it
happen. . . . Now I take limitations in stride, and with
good cheer. . . . I just let Christ take over! And so the
weaker I get, the stronger I become.*
2 Corinthians 12:9–10 MSG

The line from the children's song is reassuring: "Little ones to Him belong. They are weak but He is strong." That message applies to kids of all ages: we all are weak indeed, but we worship a mighty God.

Are you in the midst of adversity or in the stranglehold of suffering? If so, turn to God for strength. You can do all things when you rely on the power of Christ flowing through you (see Philippians 4:13). Your challenge, then, is to rely on Him. Put God at the very center of your life, and trust Him to take care of all the other stuff that surrounds you. Let Christ's strength take over where you are weak, and you'll know true power: God's power.

*God's grace and power seem to reach their peak
when we are at our weakest point.*
Anne Graham Lotz

Family Life

Above all, put on love—the perfect bond of unity.
Colossians 3:14 HCSB

Family life is a mixture of conversations, mediations, irritations, deliberations, commiserations, negotiations, and celebrations. In the life of every family, there are moments of frustration and disappointment. Lots of them. But for those fortunate enough to belong to a close-knit, caring clan, the rewards far outweigh the difficulties. That's why we pray fervently for our family members, and that's why we love them despite their faults.

No family is perfect. But in spite of the challenges and occasional hurt feelings you encounter among relatives, your family is God's gift to you. That little band of men, women, and children is a priceless treasure on loan from your heavenly Father. Take a moment today to thank Him for the gift of family . . . and to let your family members know you love and appreciate them, too.

Creating a warm, caring, supportive, encouraging environment is probably the most important thing you can do for your family.
Stephen Covey

Forgiving Those Who've Hurt You

Peter came to Him and said, "Lord, how often shall
my brother sin against me, and I forgive him?
Up to seven times?" Jesus said to him, "I do not say to you,
up to seven times, but up to seventy times seven."
Matthew 18:21–22 NKJV

How often must we forgive those who wrong us in some way? More times than we can count. Our children are precious but imperfect; so are our spouses, our parents, and our friends. Inevitably, those close to us will hurt or offend us as we travel life's road together. When they do, we must find it in our hearts to forgive them; to do otherwise is to disobey God.

Are you easily frustrated by the imperfections of others? Have you let past offenses imprison you in bitterness and anger? If so, ask God to heal your hurts and help you to forgive those who inflicted them. Bitterness and anger are not part of God's plan for your life. Forgiveness is.

Today, if there exists even one person, alive or dead, whom you have not forgiven (and that includes yourself), follow God's commandment and His will for your life: forgive.

God forgets the past. Imitate him.
Max Lucado

Anonymous Generosity

*Be careful not to do your "acts of righteousness"
before men, to be seen by them. If you do,
you will have no reward from your Father in heaven.*
Matthew 6:1 NIV

Hymn writer Fanny Crosby wrote, "To God be the glory; great thing He hath done!" But when we perform good deeds, it's tempting to claim the glory for ourselves . . . tempting, but wrong.

God's Word offers specific instruction about how we should conduct our good deeds: the glory must go to God, not to us. All praise belongs to the Creator, who inspires and enables us to do good in the first place. We are simply conduits for His generosity, and as such, we must remain humble. Otherwise, we'll forfeit the spiritual rewards that would be ours—and that God wants us to enjoy.

So the next time you perform an act of kindness or generosity, give credit where credit is due: to God.

Pride makes us artificial, and humility makes us real.
Thomas Merton

God's Eternal Presence

The world with its lust is passing away,
but the one who does God's will remains forever.
1 John 2:17 HCSB

God is ever present and everlasting. He has created the universe—and everything in it—out of nothingness. God's hand is everywhere we have ever been, and it is everywhere we will ever be. And what should be our response to this truth, as thoughtful children of God? If we're wise, we'll reach out to Him and accept the peace, the love, the abundance, and the grace that He offers.

God is always with you, throughout every season of life—in times of celebration or sorrow, victory or defeat. Though all else will pass away, God will remain; and those who do His will are promised eternal life with Him. So why not reach out to your heavenly Father right now? When you do, you can be sure that He will reach back, and you will be blessed.

The next time you hear a baby laugh or see an ocean
wave, take note. Pause and listen
as His Majesty whispers ever so gently, "I'm here."
Max Lucado

Whose Way?

We can make our plans,
but the Lord determines our steps.
Proverbs 16:9 NLT

The popular song "My Way" is a perfectly good tune, but it's not a good guide for life. If you're looking for life's perfect prescription, you'd better forget about doing things your way and concentrate on doing things God's way.

At times, even when you're trying to do God's will, you may feel stumped and wonder, "What now, Lord?" But if you earnestly seek God's will for your life, you will find it in time.

Sometimes God's plans seem crystal clear; sometimes our vision is more cloudy; sometimes it's just not the right time for Him to reveal His plan to us. So be patient, keep searching, and keep praying. If you trust the Lord to determine your steps, He will be faithful to guide you. And in time, He will answer your prayers and make His plans known—even if it's only for the next step. Today, do things His way, and you'll be eternally glad that you did.

Nothing takes God by surprise.
Everything is moving according to a plan,
and God wants you in that plan.
Billy Graham

When Grief Visits

God, who comforts the downcast, comforted us.
2 Corinthians 7:6 NIV

Grief visits all of us who live long and love deeply. When we lose a loved one, or when we experience any other profound loss, darkness overwhelms us for a while, and we feel as though we cannot summon the strength to face another day. But with God's help, we can.

God's Word tells us that He is "close to the brokenhearted" (Psalm 34:18 NIV). In times of sadness, we can turn to Him, and He will comfort us . . . and in time He will heal our hearts.

Concentration-camp survivor Corrie ten Boom once said, "There is no pit so deep that God's love is not deeper still." Let us remember those words and live by God's promises . . . especially when the days seem dark.

Throughout the millennia Christians who have known
deep suffering have found
at the same time the gift of joy.
Suffering and joy are not mutually exclusive.
Elisabeth Elliot

Being a Mentor

The one who walks with the wise will become wise.
Proverbs 13:20 HCSB

Are you willing to be a mentor to others? If so, God will certainly smile upon your endeavors. But if you find yourself "too busy" to share your wisdom with those less experienced, take a moment to remember how willingly and lavishly God has already invested in your life. Surely you can reinvest some of His wisdom and kindness in those He has placed in your path.

Think back on the parents, grandparents, family members, teachers, and friends whom God has used to bless you. Think about the impact these men and women have had on your life. Then think about your own contribution to the lives of the people who surround you today. Are you making a contribution to their lives? If so, you're keeping up your end of the bargain. If not, look for ways today that you can be a blessing to others by mentoring them. Some of that blessing will most certainly flow back to you.

You can't light another's path without
casting light on your own.
John Maxwell

Another Day,
Another Opportunity

As we have opportunity, we must work for the good of all,
especially for those who belong to the household of faith.
Galatians 6:10 HCSB

Each morning, we wade out into a vast sea of opportunities to serve God and to worship Him. When we make the most of those opportunities, He blesses us. But sometimes we feel as though we're too busy and squander those opportunities. We cheat ourselves and others out of the blessings God wants to provide.

Daily demands can leave us feeling overworked, overcommitted, and overwhelmed. Yet God wants us to slow down long enough to talk to Him, to praise Him, and to listen to His voice. When we do, our spirits will be calmed and our lives enriched . . . and amazingly, we'll find that He gives us the inner resources we need to bless others after all.

Another day, another glorious opportunity to place ourselves in the service of the One who is the Giver of all blessings. Don't miss it!

The responsible person seeks to make his or her whole life a
response to the question and call of God.
Dietrich Bonhoeffer

Meet the Neighbors

A Samaritan traveling down the road came to where the hurt man was. When he saw the man, he felt very sorry for him. The Samaritan went to him, poured olive oil and wine on his wounds, and bandaged them. Then he put the hurt man on his own donkey and took him to an inn where he cared for him.
Luke 10:33–34 NCV

Who are our neighbors? Jesus answered that question with the story of the good Samaritan. Our neighbors include anyone God places in our path—especially those in need.

We know that we are instructed to love our neighbors, and yet it seems there's so little time . . . and we're so busy. No matter. God's Word urges us to love our neighbors just as we love ourselves. No excuses.

This very day, you will encounter someone who needs a word of encouragement, a pat on the back, a helping hand, a heartfelt hug, or a sincere prayer. And if you don't reach out to that person, who will? So look for a neighbor in need, and then do something to help. You can make a difference in someone's life. And there's no better feeling than that.

The impersonal government can never replace the helping hand of a neighbor.
Hubert H. Humphrey

A Test of Endurance

Patient endurance is what you need now,
so that you will continue to do God's will.
Then you will receive all that he has promised.
Hebrews 10:36 NLT

If you've led a perfect life with absolutely no foul-ups, blunders, mistakes, or flops, you can skip this day's reading. But if you're like the rest of us, you know that occasional flubs and failures are part of living. They're common components of growing up and learning about life.

But some setbacks feel more devastating than others. That's when we must remember that even when we experience bitter disappointments, we must never lose faith. When times are tough, the Bible teaches us to keep going, to endure—and it promises God's blessing when we do. What's required of us is not perfection, only perseverance.

So if you've encountered some difficulties lately, remember that God is with you, and He will help you through. Keep doing God's will, and you'll receive all that He has promised.

Every achievement worth remembering is stained with the
blood of diligence and scarred by
the wounds of disappointment.
Charles Swindoll

Persistent Prayers

Rejoice in hope; be patient in affliction;
be persistent in prayer.
Romans 12:12 HCSB

Prayer is a powerful tool for changing your life and your world. Are you using that powerful tool to improve your world, daily interceding for people and petitioning God to have His way in the course of events? Or are you praying sporadically at best? If you're wise, you've learned that the tool of prayer is most powerful when it used often.

Today, if you haven't already done so, spend time in prayer. Establish the habit of praying constantly. Don't just pray day to day, pray hour to hour. Start each day with prayer, end it with prayer, and fill it with prayer. That's the best way to know God; it's the best way to change your world; and it is, quite simply, the best way to live.

Jesus taught that perseverance is the essential element in
prayer.
E. M. Bounds

Help with Habits

Good-hearted people, make praise your habit.
Psalm 64:9 MSG

If you sincerely desire to improve your spiritual, physical, emotional, or financial health—and if you want to make those improvements stick—then it's time to take an honest look at your habits.

Are you eating unhealthy foods? Ask God to help you make better choices. Do you smoke cigarettes? Ask God to help you quit. Do you spend more money than you should? Cut up your credit cards and ask God to give you wisdom to use wisely the resources He's given you. Do you focus on the negative aspects of your life? Redirect your thoughts to the many blessings God has given you, and meditate on His many promises.

Our habits make up the fabric of our days, and our days make up the fabric of our lives. If you develop the habit of prayer and trust in God, He'll help you break the bad habits and establish new ones that will bring blessings, not problems.

Since behaviors become habits,
make them work with you and not against you.
E. Stanley Jones

Your Worst Critic

A devout life does bring wealth,
but it's the rich simplicity of being yourself before God.
1 Timothy 6:6 MSG

Are you your own worst critic? If so, perhaps you should try being a little more understanding of the person you see when you look into the mirror.

Millions of words have been printed about ways to improve self-image and increase self-esteem. But developing and maintaining a truly healthy self-image is largely a matter of doing three things: (1) behaving ourselves as God tells us we should; (2) thinking healthy thoughts—including being grateful for the many ways God has blessed us; and (3) finding a purpose in life that pleases our Creator and ourselves.

A healthy self-image doesn't depend on what we own or what we wear or where we live. It depends on seeing ourselves as God does. God accepts us and loves us just as we are. We can be ourselves with Him—and that's a rich gift indeed.

One cannot give what he does not possess.
To give love, you must possess love.
To love others, you must love yourself.
Leo Buscaglia

September

A Joyful Journey

I've told you these things for a purpose:
that my joy might be your joy, and your joy wholly mature.
John 15:11 MSG

Complete spiritual maturity can't be achieved in a day, or in a year, or even in a lifetime. The path to spiritual maturity is never-ending; it continues, day by day, throughout every stage of life.

During every season of life, we all have opportunities to grow closer to our Creator. And if we're wise, we continue to seek God's guidance as each new chapter of life unfolds. If we cease to grow, either emotionally or spiritually, we do ourselves a profound disservice. But if we focus our thoughts—and attune our hearts—to the will of God, we'll make each day another stage in the spiritual journey . . . and as our spirits grow, so will our joy.

When it comes to walking with God,
there is no such thing as instant maturity.
God doesn't mass produce His saints.
He hand tools each one,
and it always takes longer than we expected.
Charles Swindoll

Giving Thanks

Whatever you do, in word or in deed,
do everything in the name of the Lord Jesus,
giving thanks to God the Father through Him.
Colossians 3:17 HCSB

We know we should be thankful. But sometimes, when our hearts are troubled or our spirits are crushed, we don't feel very thankful. Yet even when the clouds of despair darken our lives, God promises us His love, His strength, and His grace. That's certainly cause for us to thank Him during both good times and trying times.

Have you thanked God today for His many blessings? If you're honest, you'll have to admit that He's really given you more than you can count. In return, will you offer Him your heartfelt prayers and your wholehearted praise? If you haven't already, take time now to slow down and offer a prayer of thanksgiving to the One who has given you life on earth and life eternal.

When it comes to life, the critical thing is
whether you take things for granted
or take them with gratitude.
G. K. Chesterton

The Truth

*You shall know the truth,
and the truth shall make you free.*
John 8:32 NKJV

God is integrally linked with truth. His Word teaches the truth; His Spirit reveals the truth; His Son leads us to the truth. When we open our hearts to God, He reveals Himself, and we come to understand the truth about ourselves and the Truth (with a capital *T*) about God and His gift of grace.

The familiar words of John 8:32 remind us that when we come to know God's truth, we are liberated. Have you been liberated by that truth? Are you living in accordance with the eternal truths you find in God's Word?

Today, as you go about the tasks God has placed before you, ask yourself this question: "Do my thoughts and actions bear witness to the ultimate truth that God has placed in my heart, or am I allowing the pressures of everyday life to overwhelm me?" Determine to line your life up with God's truth . . . and you'll be truly free.

*The difficult truth about truth is that it often requires us
to change our perspectives,
attitudes, and rules for living.*
Susan Lenzkes

Lifetime Learning

Wisdom is sweet to your soul; if you find it,
there is a future hope for you,
and your hope will not be cut off.
Proverbs 24:14 NIV

Whether you're twelve or a hundred and twelve, you've still got lots to learn. Even if you're a wise person, there's plenty more that you need to know. Lifetime learning is part of God's plan, and He hasn't finished teaching you important lessons.

Do you want to live a life of righteousness and wisdom? If so, continue studying the ultimate source of wisdom: the Word of God. Choose to associate, day in and day out, with honorable and wise men and women. Listen to the still, small voice of God's Spirit whispering direction as you strive to act in accordance with His leading. And pray for God's guidance today and every day of your life. When you do these things, you'll keep growing both intellectually and spiritually, gaining wisdom that is sweet to your soul.

Knowledge is horizontal. Wisdom is vertical;
it comes down from above.
Billy Graham

God's Power to Change You

Now we look inside, and what we see is that anyone
united with the Messiah gets a fresh start, is created new.
The old life is gone; a new life burgeons! Look at it!
2 Corinthians 5:17 MSG

God has the power to transform your life—and He promises to do just that if you'll let Him. It's up to you, then, to decide whether to allow the Creator's transforming power to work in you and through you.

God stands at the door of your heart and waits; all you must do is to invite Him in. When you do so, the beautiful truth is, you cannot remain unchanged.

Is there some aspect of your life you'd like to change—a bad habit, an unhealthy relationship, or an unfulfilled dream? Ask God to change your heart and guide your path. Talk specifically to your heavenly Father about the person you are today and the person you want to become tomorrow. When you sincerely petition, trust, and follow Him, you'll be amazed at the things that He and you, working together, can accomplish.

In the midst of the pressure and the heat,
I am confident His hand is on my life, developing my
faith until I display His glory, transforming me into a
vessel of honor that pleases Him!
Anne Graham Lotz

The Power of Optimism

Be careful what you think,
because your thoughts run your life.
Proverbs 4:23 NCV

Have you formed the habit of thinking positive thoughts? It's a wonderful habit to acquire. Once you learn to think positively about your world and yourself, expecting the best, you're much more likely to achieve the best.

You can choose the quality, the tone, and the direction of your thoughts. You can learn to prune out the negative ones and let the positive ones flourish. And you can start today! Determine to think optimistically about your life and your future. Trust your heavenly Father and His promises. Dwell on your hopes, not your fears. Take time to celebrate God's glorious creation. And then, when you've filled your heart with hope and gladness, share your optimism with those around you!

Positive anything is better than negative nothing.
Elbert Hubbard

Filled by the Spirit

I will put my Spirit in you and you will live.
Ezekiel 37:14 NIV

Are you burdened by the pressures of everyday living? Would you like to ease that pressure but aren't sure how you can do it? Try allowing God's Spirit to fill you and to do His work in your life.

When you're filled with the Spirit, your words and deeds will reflect a love and devotion to God. When God's Spirit dwells in you, the steps of your life's journey are guided by the Creator of the universe. When you allow the Spirit to work in you and through you, you will be energized and transformed.

So today, take God up on His promise to put His Spirit in you, and you'll be amazed at just how fully you can live!

The Holy Spirit is the secret of the power in my life.
All I have to do is surrender my life to Him.
Kathryn Kuhlman

God's Offer of Strength

The LORD is the strength of my life.
Psalm 27:1 KJV

Are you running just a little short on willpower? If so, perhaps you haven't yet asked God to give you the strength you need to meet—and defeat—the bad habits that are troubling you.

God offers His power to thoughtful folks (like you) who are wise enough to ask for His strength, His protection, and His guidance in life.

If your own power has failed you on numerous occasions, turn your weaknesses over to God. If you've been having trouble standing on your own two feet, perhaps it's time to drop to your knees. If you feel stuck on the side of a mountain that seems too steep to climb, ask God to carry you. When you ask sincerely, in faith, and without reservation, He will answer. So today, ask the Lord of life to be the strength of your life.

God conquers only what we yield to Him.
Yet, when He does, and when our surrender is complete,
He fills us with a new strength that we could never have
known by ourselves. His conquest is our victory!
Shirley Dobson

When Calamity Strikes

Why am I so depressed? Why this turmoil within me?
Put your hope in God, for I will still praise Him,
my Savior and my God.
Psalm 42:11 HCSB

When calamity strikes anywhere in the world, we're often confronted with real-time images of that tragedy . . . and those images can breed anxiety. As we stare transfixed at our television screens, we may fall prey to fear, discouragement, worry, or all three. But our Father in heaven has promised us peace. God has promised that we may lead lives of abundance, not anxiety. In fact, His Word tells us to "be anxious for nothing" (Philippians 4:6 NASB). But how can we put our fears to rest? By taking those fears to God and leaving them there, trusting that He will take care of them . . . and of us.

When you find yourself becoming anxious, stop and take a moment to turn your concerns over to your heavenly Father. The same God who created the universe will comfort you if you ask Him . . . so ask Him, and trust Him. And then watch in amazement as your anxieties melt into the warmth of His loving embrace.

The cares of today are seldom those of tomorrow.
William Cowper

Sharing Your Burdens

The LORD himself goes before you and will be with you;
he will never leave you nor forsake you.
Do not be afraid; do not be discouraged.
Deuteronomy 31:8 NIV

Tough times will come, but the good news is this: they are temporary. God's love, however, is not temporary—His love endures forever. So what does that mean to you? Just this: from time to time, everyone faces hardships and disappointments, and so will you; but when hard times come your way, God stands ready to help you, protect you, and to heal you. You can take your burdens to Him.

Whatever the size of your burden, God is bigger. Ask for His help today, with faith and with fervor. Instead of worrying about your problems, turn them over to God in prayer. Instead of fretting over your next decision, ask God to lead the way. Don't be afraid or discouraged; cast your burdens upon the One who has promised to be with you always.

We are not called to be burden-bearers,
but cross-bearers and light-bearers.
We must cast our burdens on the Lord.
Corrie ten Boom

Choices, Choices, Choices

Don't depend on your own wisdom.
Respect the LORD and refuse to do wrong.
Proverbs 3:7 NCV

Life is a series of choices. Each day, we make countless decisions that can bring us closer to God or draw us away from Him. When we live according to God's commandments, we put ourselves in a position to receive the abundance and peace He offers to those who honor Him by obeying His Word. But when we turn our backs on God by disobeying Him, we create needless troubles for ourselves and our families.

Do you desire spiritual abundance and peace? God has promised to give you those gifts: simply invite Him into your heart and live according to His teachings. And when you confront a difficult decision or a powerful temptation, seek God's wisdom and depend on it. He'll help you make the right choice.

Destiny is not a matter of chance.
It is a matter of choice.
It is not a thing to be waited for;
it is a thing to be achieved.
William Jennings Bryan

Spiritual Crises

The wisdom that is from above is first pure,
then peaceable, gentle, willing to yield,
full of mercy and good fruits,
without partiality and without hypocrisy.
James 3:17 NKJV

You live in a world that seeks to snare your attention and lead you away from God. Each time you're tempted to distance yourself from the Creator, you face a spiritual crisis. A few of these crises may be monumental in scope, but most will involve the small, everyday decisions of life. In fact, life can be seen as one test after another—and with each crisis comes yet another opportunity to grow closer to God . . . if you choose to adhere to His plan for your life.

Today you will face many opportunities to say yes to your heavenly Father—and you'll encounter many opportunities to say no to Him. How you respond will determine not just the quality of your day but the direction of your life. Walk the wise path of following God, and you'll have a life full of mercy and all the good things God's wisdom brings.

Every time you make a choice, you are turning the central
part of you, the part that chooses, into something a little
different from what it was before.
C. S. Lewis

Big Dreams

*Live full lives, full in the fullness of God. God can do
anything, you know—far more than you could ever imagine
or guess or request in your wildest dreams! He does it not
by pushing us around but by working within us,
his Spirit deeply and gently within us.*
Ephesians 3:19–20 MSG

How big are you willing to dream? Are you willing to entertain the possibility that God has big plans and great things in store for you? Or are you convinced that your future is so dim that you'd better wear night goggles? If you trust God's promises, then you'll have faith that your future is intensely and eternally bright.

It takes courage to dream big dreams. And you'll discover that courage when you do three things: accept the past, trust God to handle the future, and make the most of the time He has given you today.

Nothing is too difficult for God, and no dreams are too big for Him. So start living—and dreaming—accordingly.

*You pay God a compliment
by asking great things of Him.*
Saint Teresa of Avila

A Shining Example

You are the light that gives light to the world. . . .
In the same way, you should be a light for other people.
Live so that they will see the good things you do
and will praise your Father in heaven.
Matthew 5:14, 16 NCV

Whether we like it or not, all of us are examples. The question is not whether we will be examples to our families and friends; the question is simply what kind of examples we will be.

What kind of example are you? Are you the kind of person whose life serves as a powerful example of righteousness? Does your behavior serve as a positive role model for young people? Are you a person whose actions, day in and day out, are based on integrity, fidelity, and a love for the Lord? If so, you are not only blessed by God, but you're also a powerful force for good in a world that desperately needs positive influences such as yours. You are a light through which God shines His love on the world; keep shining!

Example is not the main thing in
influencing others—it is the only thing.
Albert Schweitzer

Starting Small

*Work hard so you can present yourself to God
and receive his approval. Be a good worker,
one who does not need to be ashamed
and who correctly explains the word of truth.*
2 Timothy 2:15 NLT

Some businesses are started on a shoestring, but his was started out of a shoebox. That's where J. C. Hall kept the picture postcards that he sold in Kansas City way back in 1910. Soon Hall was joined by his brothers, and they built the business that became known as Hallmark Cards.

Today the company that Hall started in a shoebox is the largest greeting card manufacturer in the world—which just goes to show that everyone has to start someplace. So never sell yourself short, even if you're operating on a shoestring. Work hard and trust God. Because as J. C. Hall demonstrated, big things can start in small packages.

Begin to be now what you will be hereafter.
Saint Jerome

Finding Fulfillment

You haven't done this before.
Ask, using my name, and you will receive,
and you will have abundant joy.
John 16:24 NLT

Everywhere we turn, it seems, there are promises of fulfillment, contentment, and happiness. But the happiness the world offers is fleeting and incomplete. Thankfully, the contentment God offers is truly fulfilling—and everlasting.

Happiness depends less on our circumstances than on the attitude of our heart and mind. When we turn our thoughts to God, meditate on His promises, give thanks for His gifts, and bask in His glorious creation, we'll experience the joy that God intends for His beloved children.

Do you want to find lasting fulfillment? Don't turn to the world. Turn to God and ask Him to provide all that you need. He has promised to fill your life with abundant joy, and He always keeps His promises.

The secret of a happy life is to
do your duty and trust in God.
Sam Jones

God's Will and Ours

There is no wisdom, understanding, or advice
that can succeed against the LORD.
Proverbs 21:30 NCV

God has will, and so do we. He gave us the power to make decisions for ourselves, and He created a world in which our choices have consequences.

When we align our will with God's instructions, and when we make choices that are in accordance with His will, we'll receive His blessings of peace and joy. But if we struggle against God's will for our lives, we may reap an unhappy harvest indeed.

Today you'll face thousands of small choices; use God's Word as your guide. And as you make the bigger decisions, talk to God and seek His direction. When you trust Him implicitly and follow Him faithfully, you'll discover that God's plan is far grander than any you could have imagined.

Joy is not gush; joy is not mere jolliness.
Joy is perfect acquiescence, acceptance,
and rest in God's will, whatever comes.
Amy Carmichael

Surrounded by Love

> *Unfailing love surrounds those who trust the LORD.*
> *Psalm 32:10 NLT*

Saint Augustine said, "God loves each of us as if there were only one of us." Do you believe those words? Do you seek to have an intimate, one-on-one relationship with your heavenly Father, or are you satisfied to keep Him at a "safe" distance?

Sometimes, amid the flurry of our daily duties, God may seem far away; but He is not. God is everywhere—not only right beside us but all around us. He is with us night and day; He knows our thoughts and our emotions. He hears every prayer. And when we earnestly seek Him, we will find Him—He's waiting patiently for us to reach out to Him.

Reach out to Him today and always. He will surround you with a love that never fails . . . and that's a promise.

> *I have learned that the more we understand how very much God loves us, and the more we comprehend the grace He has demonstrated toward us, the more humble we become.*
> *Serita Ann Jakes*

Beyond Confusion

*Trust the LORD with all your heart, and don't depend
on your own understanding. Remember the LORD
in all you do, and he will give you success.*
Proverbs 3:5–6 NCV

The Bible contains promises, made by God, upon which we can depend. And we should. But sometimes, especially when we find ourselves caught in the everyday entanglements of living, we fail to trust God completely.

Are you tired? Discouraged? Fearful? Trust the promises God has made to you, and be comforted. Are you worried or anxious? Be confident in God's power. Does the future seem difficult? Be courageous and call upon God: He will protect you and then work in and through you according to His purposes. Are you confused? Listen to the quiet voice of your heavenly Father. He is not a God of confusion. Talk with Him; trust Him. Honor Him in all you do, and He will give you success.

*When the winds are cold, and the days are long,
And thy soul from care would hide,
Fly back, fly back, to thy Father then,
And beneath His wings abide.*
Fanny Crosby

When Waiting Is Hard

*Those that wait upon the L*ORD,
they shall inherit the earth.
Psalm 37:9 KJV

Sometimes the hardest thing to do is to wait. This is especially true when we're in a hurry and when we want things to happen now—if not sooner. But God's plan doesn't always unfold in the way we would like or with the speed we want it to. But as thoughtful men and women who trust in a benevolent, all-knowing Father, we must learn to wait patiently for God to reveal Himself and to work out His plan for our lives.

We humans know precisely what we want, and we know exactly when we want it. But we don't always know what's best. God does. He has a perfect plan for each of us. We simply need to trust Him enough to wait and let Him work it out in His perfect timing. After all, He is trustworthy, and Father always knows best.

The affairs of God are accomplished little by little and
almost imperceptibly.
The Spirit of God is neither violent nor hasty.
Saint Vincent de Paul

Wisdom and Hope

Make your ear attentive to wisdom,
incline your heart to understanding.
Proverbs 2:2 NASB

Wisdom and hope are traveling companions. Wise men and women learn to think optimistically about their lives, their futures, and their faith. Pessimists choose instead to focus their thoughts and energies on faultfinding, criticizing, and complaining.

To become wise, we must choose hope—and we must live according to God's Word. To become wise, we must seek God's guidance. We must not only learn the lessons of life, we must live by them.

Do you want the gifts of wisdom and hope? Then remember this: the ultimate source of wisdom is the Word of God. When you take God at His Word and follow His path, you will surely become wise . . . and you will never lose hope.

Troubles we bear trustfully can bring us
a fresh vision of God and a new outlook on life,
an outlook of peace and hope.
Billy Graham

Judging Others

Do not judge, or you too will be judged.
For in the same way you judge others, you will be judged,
and with the measure you use, it will be measured to you.
Matthew 7:1–2 NIV

We all have fallen short of God's standard, and He has forgiven us. So must we forgive others when they don't live up to our expectations. But even beyond forgiving, we must refrain from judging others.

It's all too easy for most of us to judge others. But God is the supreme Judge, and He does not need (or, for that matter, want) our help. He is perfectly capable of judging the human heart . . . we, however, are not equipped to judge rightly, because we cannot truly know what's in a person's heart as God does.

To judge others is to invite fearful consequences: to the extent we judge others, we will be judged by God. Let us refrain, then, from judging our neighbors. Instead, let us forgive them and love them in the same way that God has forgiven and loves us.

You have no idea how big
the other fellow's troubles are.
B. C. Forbes

Media Messages

Don't become so well-adjusted to your culture
that you fit into it without even thinking.
Instead, fix your attention on God.
Romans 12:2 MSG

Sometimes it seems as though the media industry is working around the clock in an attempt to rearrange your family's priorities in ways that are not in your best interests. The messages often teach that physical appearance is all-important, that material possessions should be acquired at almost any cost, and that the world operates independently of God's laws. But guess what? Those messages are untrue.

The media (sometimes unintentionally, sometimes quite intentionally) tend to glamorize violence, exploit suffering, and sensationalize sex. So here's a question for you and your family: will you control what appears on your TV screen, or will you be controlled by it? If you're willing to take charge of what's viewed inside the four walls of your home, you'll be doing yourself and your family a huge favor.

Today, forget the media hype and pay attention to God. You owe it to your Creator . . . and you owe it to yourselves.

We are made spiritually lethargic
by a steady diet of materialism.
Mary Morrison Suggs

Past Regrets

> *I will give you a new heart*
> *and put a new spirit within you.*
> Ezekiel 36:26 HCSB

If you're mired in the quicksand of regret, it's time to plan your escape. How can you do so? You can start by learning to accept the past and trust God with your future.

Life holds few if any rewards for those who remain angrily focused on the deeds and misdeeds of yesterday. Still, forgiving and moving on can be difficult for even the most saintly men and women. Being frail, fallible, imperfect human beings, most of us are quick to anger, quick to blame, slow to forgive, and even slower to forget. Yet God's way is for us to forgive, just as we have been forgiven.

If you have not yet made peace with your past, begin today. If you ask Him to, God will give you a new heart and put His spirit in you. Then you can then learn to move past your regrets and live contentedly and joyfully.

> *You can't have a better tomorrow*
> *if you are thinking about yesterday all the time.*
> Charles Kettering

Abundant Peace

*Abundant peace belongs to those who love
Your instruction; nothing makes them stumble.*
Psalm 119:165 HCSB

On many occasions, our outward struggles are simply manifestations of the inner conflicts that we feel when we stray from God's path. What's needed is a refresher course in God's peace.

The words of Psalm 119:165 remind us that God promises peace to those who accept His instruction. Today and every day, count yourself among that number. Study God's promises carefully and trust them completely. When you do, you will be a beacon of light, hope, and wisdom to your family and to your world.

So don't focus too intently on the frustrations of everyday living. Instead, invite God to preside over every aspect of your life. It's the best way to live and the surest path to peace . . . today and forever.

*Have courage for the great sorrows of life and patience
for the small ones, and when you have laboriously
accomplished your daily task,
go to sleep in peace. God is awake.*
Victor Hugo

God's Marvelous Works

Be thankful to Him, and bless His name.
For the LORD is good; His mercy is everlasting,
and His truth endures to all generations.
Psalm 100:4–5 NKJV

In the Hebrew version of the Old Testament, the title of the book of Psalms is translated "hymns of praise," and with good reason. Much of the book is a breathtakingly beautiful celebration of God's power, love, and creation. The psalmist wrote, "Let everything that breathes praise the LORD. Hallelujah!" (150:6 HCSB).

We should continually praise God for all He has done and all He will do. His works are marvelous, His gifts are exceedingly wonderful, and His love endures forever.

Do you sincerely desire to be a worshipper of the One who has given you eternal love and eternal life? Then meditate on His marvelous works. Ponder His promises. And praise Him, not just on Sunday morning but all day long, every day, for as long as you live . . . and then for all eternity.

Praise Him! Praise Him! Tell of His excellent greatness.
Praise Him! Praise Him! Ever in joyful song!
Fanny Crosby

Putting Off Procrastination

Now, Lord, what do I wait for? My hope is in You.
Psalm 39:7 HCSB

Procrastination takes a twofold toll on its victims. First, important work goes unfinished; second (and more importantly), valuable energy is wasted in the effort of putting things off. Procrastination is our shortsighted attempt to postpone some temporary discomfort. What results is a senseless cycle of delay, followed by worry, followed by a panicky and often futile attempt to "catch up." Procrastination, at its core, is a struggle against oneself; and the only antidote is action.

Once you acquire the habit of doing what needs to be done when it needs to be done, you'll avoid untold trouble, worry, and stress. So learn to put off procrastination by paying less attention to your fears and more attention to your responsibilities. Put your hope in God, and He'll help you tackle whatever you need to do today. Come on . . . what are you waiting for?

Know the true value of time!
Snatch, seize, and enjoy every moment of it.
No idleness, no laziness, no procrastination.
Never put off till tomorrow what you can do today.
Lord Chesterfield

Playing It Safe

Cast your burden upon the LORD and He will sustain you:
He will never allow the righteous to be shaken.
Psalm 55:22 NASB

As we consider the uncertainties of the future, we may be confronted with a powerful temptation to "play it safe." Unwilling to move mountains, we fret over molehills. Unwilling to entertain great hopes for the tomorrow, we focus on the frustrations of today. Unwilling to trust God completely, we take timid halfsteps when God is urging us to take giant leaps of faith.

Today, ask God for the courage to step beyond the boundaries your doubts would set. Ask Him to guide you to a place where you can realize your full potential—a place where you are free from the fear of failure. Ask Him to do His part, and promise Him that you will do your part. Don't ask God to lead you to a "safe" place; ask Him to lead you to the "right" place. And never fear: the One who sustains the universe will sustain you.

The really committed leave the safety of the harbor, accept
the risk of the open seas of faith, and set their compasses
for the place of total devotion to God and whatever life
adventures He plans for them.
Bill Hybels

The Benefits of Obedience

If you hide your sins, you will not succeed.
If you confess and reject them, you will receive mercy.
Proverbs 28:13 NCV

As creatures of free will, we can rebel against God whenever we choose; but when we do, we put ourselves at risk. Why? Because God promises to protect those who obey Him, but He also warns that disobedience invites disaster.

Thankfully, God offers forgiveness to all who seek it (see Psalm 145:9; Psalm 103:2–3). And He offers peace to those who ask (see Luke 11:9; John 14:27). When we honor God by obeying His commandments, He blesses us in ways that are sometimes obvious and sometimes subtle.

Would you like a proven prescription for successful living, a formula based on the rock-solid foundation of God's promises? Here it is: Study God's Word and, to the best of your abilities, live by it. When you do, you'll discover that the Creator supplies a bountiful harvest to people (like you) who have the wisdom and the discipline to obey Him.

A divine strength is given to those who yield themselves to the Father
and obey what He tells them to do.
Warren Wiersbe

Your Unique Talents

There are varieties of gifts, but the same Spirit.
And there are varieties of ministries, and the same Lord.
1 Corinthians 12:4–5 NASB

God has given you a unique set of skills, and He has given you countless opportunities to share those gifts with the world. Your Creator intends for you to use your talents for His glory and His kingdom, in the service of His children. Will you honor Him by using your skills as He directs? Will you share His gifts humbly and lovingly? If you use your talents to the full, you can be sure God will bless you and reward your efforts.

Make this promise to yourself and to God: that you will use your talents to minister to your family, to your friends, and to the world. And while you're at it, remember this: God's gifts to you are on loan, and He expects you to return them with interest . . . so start investing today.

One well-cultivated talent, deepened and enlarged,
is worth one hundred shallow faculties.
William Matthews

October

While It Is Day

I must work the works of Him who sent Me
while it is day; the night is coming when no one can work.
John 9:4 NKJV

The words of John 9:4 remind us that "night is coming" for all of us. But when we take God at His Word—and when we take comfort in His promises—we need never fear the night. After all, the Father has promised to love us and protect us. Armed with these assurances, we can face life courageously, seizing the opportunities He places before us each day.

Today is a priceless gift that has been given to you by God—don't waste it. Don't stand on the sidelines as life's parade passes you by. Instead, search for the possibilities God has placed along your path. This day is a one-of-a-kind treasure that can be put to good use—or wasted. Your challenge is to use this day joyfully and productively. And while you're at it, encourage others to do likewise. After all, night is coming.

Live today fully, expressing gratitude
for all you have been, all you are right now,
and all you are becoming.
Melodie Beattie

God with Us

When you go through deep waters, I will be with you.
When you go through rivers of difficulty, you will not
drown. When you walk through the fire of oppression, you
will not be burned up; the flames will not consume you.
For I am the LORD, your God.
Isaiah 43:2–3 NLT

From time to time, all of us face adversity, discouragement, or disappointment. But we need never face our troubles alone. God has promised to walk with us as we journey into—and through—our hardships. And we can trust the Father to keep His promises. When we're troubled, we can call upon God, and in His own time and according to His own plan, He will restore us.

Are you anxious? Take those anxieties to God. Are you troubled? Take your troubles to Him. Does your world seem to be crumbling around you? Seek protection from the One who cannot be moved. The same God who created the universe will protect you if you ask Him . . . so ask Him, and know that God is with you.

Weave the fabric of God's Word through your heart and
mind. It will hold strong, even if the rest of life unravels.
Gigi Graham Tchividjian

Actions and Beliefs

If the way you live isn't consistent with what you believe,
then it's wrong.
Romans 14:23 MSG

We must do our best to make sure that our actions are accurate reflections of our beliefs. Our theology must manifest itself not only in our words but, more importantly, in our actions. In short, we should be practical people, quick to act upon the beliefs we hold most dear.

We can proclaim our beliefs to our hearts' content, but our proclamations will mean nothing—to others or to ourselves—unless we accompany our words with deeds that match. The sermons we live are far more compelling than the ones we preach.

Like it or not, your life is a reflection of your creed. If this fact gives you cause for concern, don't bother talking about the changes that you intend to make—just make them, starting today.

I don't care what a man says he believes
with his lips. I want to know with a vengeance
what he says with his life and his actions.
Sam Jones

When It's Time for a Different Plan

Be strong; don't be discouraged,
for your work has a reward.
2 Chronicles 15:7 HCSB

Some of our most important dreams are the ones we abandon. Some of our most important goals are the ones we don't attain. Sometimes our most important journeys are the ones we take to the winding conclusion of what seem to be dead ends. Thankfully, with God there are no dead ends; there are only opportunities to learn, to yield, to trust, to serve, and to grow.

The next time you experience one of life's disappointments, don't despair—and don't be afraid to try Plan B. Consider every setback an opportunity to choose a different path, one that's wiser or more appropriate or just more attainable. Have faith that God may indeed be leading you in an entirely different direction, a direction of His choosing. And as you take your next step, remember that what looks like a dead end to you may, in fact, be the fast lane according to God.

Goals are worth setting and worth missing.
We learn from non-successes.
Bill Bright

Finding Contentment

I know what it is to be in need, and I know what it is
to have plenty. I have learned the secret of being content
in any and every situation, whether well fed or hungry,
whether living in plenty or in want. I can do everything
through him who gives me strength.
Philippians 4:12–13 NIV

The preoccupation with happiness and contentment seems ever-present. We're bombarded
with messages that tell us where to find peace and
pleasure in a world that worships materialism and
wealth. But lasting contentment is not found in
material possessions; genuine contentment is a
spiritual gift from God, and it's promised to those
who trust in Him and follow His commandments.

Where do we find contentment? If we don't find
it in God, we'll never find it anywhere else. But if
we put our faith and our trust in Him, we will be
blessed with an inner peace that goes beyond human
understanding. When God dwells at the center of
our lives, peace and contentment will belong to us
just as surely as we belong to God.

True contentment is a real and active virtue—
not only affirmative but creative. It is the power
of getting out of any situation all there is in it.
G. K. Chesterton

Reclaiming Life

Blessed are those who mourn,
because they will be comforted.
Matthew 5:4 HCSB

Life is made up of a series of events, some joyous and some tragic. When we face the inevitable disappointments and heartbreaks that come with living, we have several choices. We can deny our heartbreak and pretend nothing has happened; we can become embittered and lock ourselves into memories of a broken past; we can give in to our fears and allow emotional paralysis to become the hallmark of our existence; or we can accept the reality of our situation and begin moving forward as best we can.

Acceptance of a disheartening situation should never be confused with "giving in." Far from it. In fact, it's only when we face the reality of a difficult situation that we are truly free to begin changing it. So if your heart has been broken by a tragedy, either great or small, it's okay to mourn . . . for a while. But then renew your focus on God's promises and get about the business of reclaiming your life.

God whispers to us in our pleasures,
speaks in our conscience,
but shouts in our pain.
C. S. Lewis

In Good Spirits

A word spoken at the right time
is like golden apples on a silver tray.
Proverbs 25:11 HCSB

Hope, like other human emotions, is contagious. If you associate with hope-filled, enthusiastic people, their positive spirits will have a tendency to lift your spirit, too. But if you find yourself spending too much time in the company of naysayers, pessimists, or cynics, your thoughts, like theirs, will tend toward the negative.

Are you a hopeful, optimistic person? And do you associate with like-minded people? If so, then you're availing yourself of a priceless gift: the encouragement of others. Today, look for reasons to celebrate God's endless blessings. And while you're at it, look for people who will join with you in the celebration. You'll be better for their company, and they'll be better for yours.

When someone does something good, applaud!
You'll make two people feel good.
Sam Goldwyn

Faith That Works

In the gospel a righteousness from God is revealed,
a righteousness that is by faith from first to last,
just as it is written:
"The righteous will live by faith."
Romans 1:17 NIV

Through every stage of your life—during good times and bad, when you win great victories and when you suffer bitter defeats—God stands by your side, ready to strengthen you and protect you . . . if you have faith in Him.

Today, make certain that your faith is a faith that works. How? Strengthen your faith through worship, through Bible study, and through prayer. And the more you get to know God, the more you'll learn to trust His promises and His plans. With Him, all things are possible, and He stands ready to open a world of opportunities to you and yours . . . if you have faith.

Faith is not just believing; faith is being open
to what God is doing,
being willing to learn and grow.
Mary Morrison Suggs

Playing It Safe

I will not be afraid, because the Lord is my helper.
People can't do anything to me.
Hebrews 13:6 NCV

Have you spent too much time playing it safe? Are you stuck inside your comfort zone? Would you like to change the quality and direction of your life, but you're not sure how . . . or you're afraid to venture out? If you answered these questions in the affirmative, perhaps you're more fearful of change than you need to be.

Change is often difficult and sometimes uncomfortable. But the world keeps changing, and if you're wise, you'll learn to accept change as well—even to embrace it as a gift from God.

So the next time you're facing a big decision that involves a major modification in your own circumstances, trust God and summon the courage to step outside your comfort zone. Instead of fighting change, embrace it and make the best of it. Here in the real world, time doesn't stand still. And neither should you.

Take a chance. All of life is a chance.
Dale Carnegie

Cultivating God's Gifts

I remind you to fan into flame the gift of God.
2 Timothy 1:6 NIV

All people possess special gifts and talents—including you. But your gift is no guarantee of success. It must be cultivated and nurtured; otherwise, it will go unused, and God's gift to you may even be lost . . . forever.

You are the only person on earth who can use your particular talents. And make no mistake: the world needs your contributions almost as badly as you need the experience of contributing.

So today, accept this challenge: Value the talent that God has given you; nourish it, make it grow, and share it with the world. Do the hard work that's necessary to convert raw talent into polished proficiency. After all, the best way to say thank you for God's gift is to use it.

Yes, we need to acknowledge our weaknesses, to confess our sins. But if we want to be active, productive participants in the realm of God, we also need to recognize our gifts, to appreciate our strengths, to build on the abilities God has given us. We need to balance humility with confidence.
Penelope Stokes

Always Faithful

*Let us hold on to the confession of our hope
without wavering, for He who promised is faithful.*
Hebrews 10:23 HCSB

The Bible makes it perfectly clear: God is always faithful. This does not mean that we, His children, are exempt from life's troubles and tragedies. It means that God will preserve us *in* our difficulties, not *from* our difficulties.

God's faithfulness is made clear in the beautiful words of the psalmist: "Yea, though I walk through the valley of the shadow of death, I will fear no evil: for thou art with me; thy rod and thy staff they comfort me" (Psalm 23:4 KJV). When we walk through life's darkest valleys, God walks with us. He is always present, always willing to lead those who are willing to follow.

Take comfort in God's faithfulness. Trust His unfailing promises, and have faith that He will lead you to a beautiful future. Follow Him today.

*Trials are not enemies of faith
but opportunities to reveal God's faithfulness.*
Barbara Johnson

God's Plan, Our Responsibilities

His master said to him,
"Well done, good and faithful slave! You were faithful
over a few things; I will put you in charge of many things.
Share your master's joy!"
Matthew 25:21 HCSB

God has promised us this: when we do our duty in small matters, He will give us additional responsibilities. Sometimes those responsibilities come when God changes the course of our lives so that we may better serve Him. Sometimes our rewards come in the form of temporary setbacks that turn out to be segues into greater victories. Sometimes God rewards us by answering no to some request we've made—so that He can say yes to a far grander blessing that we, in our limited understanding, would never have dreamed of.

If you seek to be God's servant in great matters, be faithful, be patient, and be dutiful in smaller matters. Then step back and watch as God surprises you with the spectacular creativity of His infinite wisdom and His perfect plan.

I firmly believe that as we prove ourselves to be responsible
with our resources, more and more resources will be
entrusted to us to handle faithfully.
Mary Hunt

Guarding Your Heart

Guard your heart above all else, for it is the source of life.
Proverbs 4:23 HCSB

You are near and dear to God. He loves you more than you can imagine, and He wants the very best for you. And part of that involves guarding your heart.

Every day, you are faced with choices. And in each situation, you can do the right thing . . . or not. You can be prudent . . . or not. You can be kind and generous and obedient to God . . . or not.

Today the world will offer you many opportunities to let down your guard and, by doing so, make needless mistakes that may injure you or your loved ones. So be watchful and obedient. Guard your heart by giving it to your heavenly Father; it is safe with Him.

God never called us to naïveté.
He called us to integrity. . . .
The biblical concept of integrity emphasizes mature
innocence not childlike ignorance.
Beth Moore

Fear of Rejection

Be strong and brave, and do the work. Don't be afraid or discouraged, because the LORD God, my God, is with you. He will not fail you or leave you.
1 Chronicles 28:20 NCV

The fear of rejection and the fear of failure are roadblocks on the way to happiness. When we try to please everyone, we set for ourselves a goal that is unsatisfying and unworthy of our efforts.

Remember, your worth comes from God. Sure, there are a few people you should seek to please, like your family, close friends, and the person who signs your paycheck. But trying to please everyone is impossible, and it's not even what God expects—especially when it comes to choosing between people-pleasing and keeping the faith. Your top priority should be to please your heavenly Father. Then, even if others reject you, He will accept you and reward you with eternal life.

Never allow anyone to rain on your parade and thus cast a pall of gloom and defeat on the entire day. Remember that no talent, no self-denial, no brains, no character, are required to set up in the fault-finding business. Nothing external can have any power over you unless you permit it.
Og Mandino

Positive Thoughts
and a Happy Heart

Happy are those who keep His decrees
and seek Him with all their heart.
Psalm 119:2 HCSB

Happiness depends less upon our circumstances than upon our own thoughts and actions. When we thank God for His gifts and rejoice in His glorious creation, those positive thoughts bring their own rewards. But when we focus on the negative aspects of life, we invite needless suffering into our lives and those around us.

The Roman poet Horace noted, "You traverse the world in search of happiness, which is within reach of every person—a contented mind confers it all." These words remind us that happiness is closely connected with our thought life.

Nobody can make you happy—you have to choose it for yourself. When you turn your thoughts toward God and meditate on His wonderful promises, you'll know the joy of a happy heart.

Happiness is not a matter of events;
it depends on the tides of the mind.
Alice Meynell

Unchanging Laws

*God's Law is more real and lasting than the stars
in the sky and the ground at your feet.
Long after stars burn out and earth wears out,
God's Law will be alive and working.*
Matthew 5:18 MSG

God's laws are eternal and unchanging, and obeying them leads to abundance and joy. God has given us a guidebook for righteous living called the Bible. If we trust God's Word and live by it, we'll be blessed.

Life is a series of choices. Each day we make countless decisions, and it seems we're always faced with some new dilemma. In a world of whirlwind change, you can find sure, steady ground on which to stand when you stand on the promises and obey the instructions in God's Word.

Do you seek God's peace and His blessings? Then live by God's Law. When you're faced with a difficult choice or a powerful temptation, seek direction and wisdom from His Word—God's Law never changes, and you can trust the counsel it gives.

*Believe and do what God says. The life-changing
consequences will be limitless, and the results
will be confidence and peace of mind.*
Franklin Graham

Including God in Your Plans

*Commit your activities to the LORD
and your plans will be achieved.*
Proverbs 16:3 HCSB

Would you like a formula for successful living that never fails? Here it is: include God in every aspect of your life's journey, including all the plans you make and each step you take. But beware: as you make plans for the days and weeks ahead, it's all too easy to become sidetracked by the chores of everyday living.

If you allow the world to establish your priorities, you'll eventually become discouraged, disappointed, or both. But if you genuinely seek God's will for every important decision you make, your loving, heavenly Father will guide your steps and enrich your life. So as you plan your work, remember that every good plan should start with God.

God has a plan for your life . . . do you?
Marie T. Freeman

On Purpose

*Your Father knows exactly what
you need even before you ask him!*
Matthew 6:8 NLT

God's purpose for your life is not a destination to be reached; it is a path to be traveled, a journey that unfolds every day of your life. And that's exactly how often you should seek direction from your Creator: one day at a time, each day followed by the next, without exception.

Daily prayer and meditation is a matter of will and habit. We must willingly organize our time by carving out quiet moments with God, and we must form the habit of daily worship. When we do, we'll discover that no time is more precious than the silent moments we spend in the company of our heavenly Father. In fact, the quality of our spiritual life will be in direct proportion to the quality of our prayer life.

Today and every day, God is listening; He wants to hear from you; and if you want to live according to His good purpose for your life, you'll need to hear from Him.

*God insists that we ask, not because He needs
to know our situation, but because we need
the spiritual discipline of asking.*
Catherine Marshall

Your Questions, God's Answers

This God is our God for ever and ever;
he will be our guide even to the end.
Psalm 48:14 NIV

When you have a question you can't answer, whom do you ask? When you face a difficult decision, to whom do you turn for counsel? To friends? To mentors? To family members? Or do you turn first to the ultimate source of wisdom? The answers to life's big questions start with God and with the wisdom and promises contained in His Word.

God's wisdom stands forever, and His Word is a light for every generation. Make it your light as well. Use the Bible as a compass on your life's journey. Use it as the yardstick by which your behavior is measured. And as you carefully consult the pages of God's Word, ask Him to reveal the wisdom you need. When you take your concerns to your heavenly Father, He will not turn you away; He will provide answers that are tested and true.

We are finding we don't have such a gnawing need to
know the answers when we know the Answer.
Gloria Gaither

God's Solution to Our Guilt

If My people who are called by My name will humble
themselves, and pray and seek My face, and turn from
their wicked ways, then I will hear from heaven,
and will forgive their sin and heal their land.
2 Chronicles 7:14 NKJV

All of us have made mistakes. Sometimes our troubles result from our own stubborn rebellion against God's commandments. Sometimes we're swept up in events that are beyond our control. Under either set of circumstances, we may experience feelings of guilt. But God has a solution for the guilt we feel. That answer is His forgiveness.

When we confess and turn away from wrongdoing, the One who created us promises to forgive us.

Are you troubled by feelings of guilt or regret? If so, repent of your misdeeds and ask your heavenly Father for forgiveness. He will forgive you completely and without reservation. Then you can—and should—forgive yourself just as God has forgiven you: thoroughly and unconditionally.

In repentance, we must show willingness
to make amends, plus willingness to do
whatever we must to avoid repeating the sin.
Shirley Dobson

On Being Still

Be still, and know that I am God.
Psalm 46:10 KJV

Are you so busy that you rush through the day with scarcely a single moment for quiet contemplation and prayer? If so, it sounds like you need to be still.

We live in a noisy world—a world filled with distractions, frustrations, and complications. But if we allow the distractions of that clamorous world to separate us from God's peace, we do ourselves a profound disservice. If we are to maintain clear minds and compassionate hearts, we must take time each day for prayer and for meditation on God's Word. We must make ourselves still in the presence of our Creator. We must quiet our minds and our hearts so that we can hear God's whisper and sense God's love.

Nothing is more important than the time you spend with your heavenly Father. After all, God may be speaking to you right now—so be still . . . and listen.

It is in that stillness that the Voice will be heard,
the only voice in all the universe that speaks peace to the
deepest part of us.
Elisabeth Elliot

Too Busy to Give Thanks

It is good to give thanks to the LORD,
to sing praises to the Most High.
It is good to proclaim your unfailing love in the morning,
your faithfulness in the evening.
Psalm 92:1–2 NLT

Life has a way of constantly coming at us. Days, hours, and moments are filled with urgent demands requiring our immediate attention.

When the demands of life leave us rushing from place to place with scarcely a moment to spare, we may fail to pause and thank our Creator for His gifts. But whenever we neglect to give proper thanks to the Giver of life and of all we have, we're the ones to suffer. Our misplaced priorities will lead to misdirected thoughts and attitudes, and that leads to missed blessings along life's path.

Today, make a special effort to give thanks to God for His blessings. When you consider His goodness to you, you'll realize you can never be too busy to give thanks.

It is only with gratitude that life becomes rich.
Dietrich Bonhoeffer

Feeding the Church

Take heed therefore unto yourselves,
and to all the flock, over the which the Holy Ghost
hath made you overseers, to feed the church of God.
Acts 20:28 KJV

The Bible teaches that we should worship God in our hearts and in our churches—we have clear instructions to "feed the church of God." The church belongs to God; it is His just as certainly as we are His. When we help to build up God's church—not the building but the body of Christ—we bear witness to the changes He has made in our lives.

Are you an active member of your own fellowship? Are you a builder of bridges inside the four walls of your church and outside it? Do you contribute your time and your talents?

God's church is intended to be a powerful tool for spreading His Good News and uplifting His children. What are you doing to be part of His church today?

Where the Church is, there is the Spirit of God;
and where the Spirit of God is, there is the Church and all
grace—and the Spirit is truth.
Saint Irenaeus

The Rewards of Work

*The one who plants and the one who waters have
the same purpose, and each will be rewarded
for his own work.*
1 Corinthians 3:8 NCV

Whether you're at work, at school, or any place
in between, your success will depend, in large
part, on the quality and quantity of your work. So
whatever you choose to do, do it with commitment,
excitement, and vigor. That's the way God has called
all of us to do the work He has set before us.

God did not create you for a life of mediocrity;
He created you for far greater things. Reaching for
greater things usually requires plenty of effort, but
that's perfectly okay with the Creator. After all, He
knows that with His help you can accomplish the
task—and He knows that hard work builds character.
So don't treat work as a burden; treat it as a sure way
to accomplish God's plans . . . and a proven way to
build a better life for you and yours.

*The happy people are those who are
producing something.*
William Ralph Inge

Worship as Part of God's Plan

*I rejoiced with those who said to me,
"Let us go to the house of the LORD."*
Psalm 122:1 HCSB

God has a wonderful plan for your life, and an important part of that plan includes worship. Let us never deceive ourselves: every life is based on some form of worship. The question is not whether we worship, but what we worship.

Some of us choose to worship God. That brings a plentiful harvest of joy, peace, and spiritual abundance. Others distance themselves from God by worshipping earthly possessions or personal gratification. And while that may bring an immediate return of material pleasures, the ultimate harvest will be devastatingly empty.

Do you enjoy God's incomparable blessings? Then worship Him, today and every day. Worship Him with sincerity and thanksgiving, and you'll know true rejoicing forever.

*We're here to be worshipers first and workers
only second. The work done by a worshiper
will have eternity in it.*
A. W. Tozer

How to Get Rich

Be careful and guard against all kinds of greed.
Life is not measured by how much one owns.
Luke 12:15 NCV

Earthly riches are temporary: here today and soon gone. Spiritual riches, on the other hand, can be ours today, tomorrow, and throughout eternity. Yet all too often we focus our thoughts and energies on the accumulation of earthly treasures, leaving precious little time to accumulate the only treasures that really matter: the spiritual kind.

Our material possessions have the potential to do great good or to bring harm, depending upon how we choose to use them. God's Word tells us to be faithful, generous stewards of the gifts He has seen fit to bestow upon us. He instructs us to focus on spiritual rewards, not earthly possessions.

So today, honor God by seeking the kind of wealth only He can offer. Put Him first in your life, and your life will be rich indeed.

When we put people before possessions
in our hearts, we are sowing seeds
of enduring satisfaction.
Beverly LaHaye

Honesty: God's Policy

Lying lips are an abomination to the LORD,
but those who deal truthfully are His delight.
Proverbs 12:22 NKJV

From the time we are children, we are taught that honesty is the best policy; but sometimes it's hard to be honest and oh, so easy to be less than honest. So we convince ourselves that it's all right to tell "little white lies." But there's a problem: little white lies tend to grow up, and when they do, they cause havoc and pain in our lives.

For spiritually minded adults, the issue of honesty is not a topic for debate. Honesty is not just the best policy; it is God's policy, pure and simple. So we must avoid all lies, white or otherwise.

Sometime soon, perhaps even today, you'll be tempted to "bend the truth," perhaps in the form of a "harmless" white lie. Resist that temptation. Truth is God's way, and "those who deal truthfully are His delight."

We must learn, then, to relate transparently
and genuinely to others because that is
God's style of relating to us.
Rebecca Manley Pippert

Acceptance and Peace

Come to terms with God and be at peace;
in this way good will come to you.
Job 22:21 HCSB

We all experience adversity and pain at some point in our lives. And as human beings with limited understanding, we can never fully understand the will of our Father in heaven, so we may not understand why He allows suffering to come into our lives. But as believers in a benevolent God, we can always trust His providence.

When Jesus went to the Mount of Olives, He poured out His heart to God. Jesus knew the agony that He was about to endure, but He also knew that God's will must be done. We, too, should embrace God's plan for our lives, even when we don't comprehend it . . . even when it's difficult.

Are you embittered by a personal tragedy that you did not deserve and cannot understand? If so, it's time to accept the unchangeable past, embrace the priceless present, and have faith in God's promises for tomorrow. His plans for you are good. Come to God and reclaim the peace—His peace—that can be yours.

Leave the broken, irreversible past in God's hands,
and step out into the invincible future with Him.
Oswald Chambers

Just Ask

He granted their request because they trusted in Him.
1 Chronicles 5:20 HCSB

Have you formed the habit of asking God for the things you need? If so, you're continually inviting your Creator to reveal Himself in a variety of ways. And as a thoughtful person who trusts God's promises, you'll want to do no less.

Do you have questions about your future? Do you have needs that you can't meet by yourself? Do you sincerely want to know God's purpose for your life? If so, ask Him for direction, for provision, for whatever it is you need—and then keep asking Him every day that you live.

Whatever your need, no matter how great or small, pray about it and never lose hope. God is with you, and He's perfectly capable of answering your prayers. It's up to you to ask.

Don't be afraid to ask your heavenly Father
for anything you need.
Indeed, nothing is too small
for God's attention or too great for His power.
Dennis Swanberg

Burning Bright
Instead of Burning Out

Don't burn out; keep yourselves fueled and aflame.
Be alert servants of the Master, cheerfully expectant.
Don't quit in hard times; pray all the harder.
Romans 12:11–12 MSG

Has the busy pace of life robbed you of the peace that might otherwise be yours? If so, it seems you're too busy for your own good.

God offers, to anyone who will accept them, His strength and peace. But He won't force His gifts on us. In order to experience these blessings, we have to slow down long enough to spend time in His presence.

Today, as a gift to yourself, to your family, and to the world, slow down and take time to let God refuel your spirit and your energy. Let Him fill you with the inner peace that comes only from Him. When times get tough, don't quit—go in prayer to the Source of all you need. With the flame of His Spirit blazing in your heart and life, you'll never burn out.

To do too much is as dangerous as to do nothing at all.
Both modes prevent us from savoring our moments.
One causes me to rush right past the best of life without
recognizing or basking in it, and the other finds me sitting
quietly as life rushes past me.
Patsy Clairmont

Working Miracles

The kingdom of God is present not in talk but in power.
1 Corinthians 4:20 NCV

In 1887, Anne Sullivan began her service as governess and instructor of a young girl named Helen Keller. A childhood illness had left Helen blind and deaf, but Anne started teaching, and Helen began learning. As her young student began to make dramatic improvements, Anne became known as "the miracle worker." But she knew that Helen's improvement was not a miracle at all; it was the result of perseverance, faith, and hard work. Anne commented, "People seldom see the halting and painful steps by which real success is achieved."

If you've been impatient for your own success, remember that your giant leap forward may be preceded by a lengthy succession of short, halting steps. But keep the faith, keep working, and keep taking those steps, even if they're small ones. If you do, the results might just be miraculous.

God specializes in things thought impossible.
Catherine Marshall

November

No Negativity

*Let's agree to use all our energy in getting along
with each other. Help others with encouraging words;
don't drag them down by finding fault.*

Romans 14:19–20 MSG

From experience, we know it's easy to criticize others. And we know it's usually far easier to find faults than to find solutions. The urge to criticize others remains a powerful temptation for most of us.

But negativity is highly contagious: we give it to others who, in turn, give it back to us. This cycle can be broken only by positive thoughts, heartfelt prayers, encouraging words, and meaningful acts of kindness.

As children of a loving God who pours out His blessings on us, we really have no valid reason—and no legitimate excuse—to be negative. So when we're tempted to be critical of others, or overly critical of ourselves, let's instead call on the transforming power of God's love to break the chains of negativity. With God's help, we can defeat negativity before negativity defeats us.

*If I long to improve my brother,
the first step toward doing so is to improve myself.*

Christina Rossetti

Faith over Feelings

The just shall live by faith.
Hebrews 10:38 NKJV

Hebrews 10:38 teaches that we should live by faith. Yet sometimes, despite our best intentions, feelings of doubt and fear can rob us of the peace and spiritual abundance that should be ours through Christ. Anger or anxiety can keep us from the blessings God wants to bestow. So we must learn to put faith over feelings. Human emotions are highly variable, decidedly unpredictable, and often unreliable. Our emotions are like the weather, only far more fickle. That's why God wants us to live by faith, not by the ups and downs of our own emotional roller coasters.

Sometime during this day, you will probably be gripped by a strong negative emotion. Distrust it. Rein it in. Test it. And turn it over to God. Our emotions change; God does not. So trust Him completely, and let your feelings slowly fade, to be replaced by faith.

*If you are going to be a person who is committed
to the Word of God, you will have to learn to be led by the
Spirit and not by your emotions.*
Joyce Meyer

Overcoming the World

Call upon me in the day of trouble:
I will deliver thee, and thou shalt glorify me.
Psalm 50:15 KJV

Today he's a respected pastor in Memphis, Tennessee. But in the 1970s, Al Green was just about as far from the church as he could get. As one of the best-selling recording artists in the world, he lived life in the fast lane, and he didn't spend much time thinking about or talking about God. But all that changed in 1977, when Green faced a personal tragedy that caused him to reassess his life and turn it over to God.

Today Reverend Green's advice is straightforward: "If you just hang in there with God, everything's gonna be all right."

1 John 5:4 says, "Whatever is born of God overcomes the world" (NKJV). So when Old Man Trouble knocks on your door, remember: if you stand with God, He'll stand by you—and together, you'll overcome whatever the world throws at you.

God's all-sufficiency is a major.
Your inability is a minor.
Major in majors, not in minors.
Corrie ten Boom

Noble Plans

A noble person plans noble things;
he stands up for noble causes.
Isaiah 32:8 HCSB

If you have no idea where you want to go, any road will take you there. And if you're determined to live a life of total spontaneity, a life devoid of planning and preparation, you never know where you'll end up. But if you're like most people, you'll find greater contentment and success if you plan for the future. In fact, a clearly marked road map for life can be a powerful tool for achieving the things you want and need. And when those plans are noble, to advance noble causes, God will bless them—and you.

Life is unpredictable, of course, but uncertainty is no excuse for fuzzy thinking or sloppy planning. Today (and throughout your life), invest ample time planning for this day and each day that follows. Seek God's guidance, and He will give it. Determine—and plan—to act nobly. Then summon the energy and the courage to implement your plans . . . and God will help you to fulfill them.

Let our advance worrying become
advance thinking and planning.
Winston Churchill

Taking Time to Enjoy

Always be full of joy in the Lord. I say it again—rejoice!
Philippians 4:4 NLT

Are you a person who takes time each day to really enjoy life? Hopefully so. After all, you are the recipient of a precious gift—the gift of life. And because God has seen fit to give you this gift, it is incumbent upon you to use it and to enjoy it. But sometimes, amid the pressures and demands of everyday living, really enjoying life may seem almost impossible.

It's not.

For most of us, fun is as much a function of attitude as it is a function of environment. So whether you're standing victorious atop one of life's mountains or trudging through one of life's valleys, enjoy yourself. You deserve to have fun today, and God wants you to enjoy the life He's given you . . . so what are you waiting for?

People who cannot find time for recreation
are obliged sooner or later to find time for illness.
John Wanamaker

Showers of Blessings

I will bless them and the places surrounding my hill.
I will send down showers in season;
there will be showers of blessing.
Ezekiel 34:26 NIV

Do you know how richly you have been blessed? Well, God's gifts are actually too numerous to count, but if you are wise, you'll inventory as many blessings as you can, as often as you can. And after you've finished that inventory, you'll find it easy and even enjoyable to give thanks to the Giver of all things good: your Father in heaven.

A thankful heart is a wise heart. Are you thankful (and thus wise), or have you been taking God's gifts for granted? If you've temporarily lost sight of God's role in the richness of your life, the best way to remedy that is by making this day (and every day) a time for celebration and praise.

Do we not continually pass by blessings innumerable
without notice, and instead fix our eyes on
what we feel to be our trials and our losses,
and think and talk about these until our whole horizon
is filled with them, and we almost begin
to think we have no blessings at all?
Hannah Whitall Smith

God's Love for You

I am persuaded that neither death nor life, nor angels nor principalities nor powers, nor things present nor things to come, nor height nor depth, nor any other created thing, shall be able to separate us from the love of God which is in Christ Jesus our Lord.
Romans 8:38–39 NKJV

When we worship God with faith and assurance, when we place Him at the absolute center of our lives, we invite His love into our hearts. And when we sense His love for us, we grow to love Him more deeply as well.

God is love, and God's love is perfect. When we open ourselves to His perfect love, we are touched by the Creator's hand and transformed, not just for a day, but for all eternity.

Today, as you carve out quiet moments of thanksgiving and praise for your heavenly Father, open yourself to His presence and to His love. He is here, waiting. His love is here, and available to all. Accept it and be blessed.

*A major turning point in my life came when
I realized that being able to trust God
is grounded in staking the whole of my being
on the reality that He loves me.*
Paula Rinehart

Expectations

I say to myself, "The LORD is mine, so I hope in him."
Lamentations 3:24 NCV

What do you expect from the day ahead? Are you expecting God to do wonderful things, or are you living under a cloud of apprehension and doubt? If you trust God's promises, you have every reason to live optimistically, even when times are tough.

What you look for in life—what you expect—greatly influences your days and your life. If your thoughts are positive, you'll be more likely to see positive things. But the reverse is also true, so you must guard your thoughts carefully.

As you face the inevitable challenges of living, you'll be wise to arm yourself with the promises of God's Word. When you do, you can expect the best, not only for the day ahead, but also for all eternity.

At least ten times every day, affirm this thought:
"I expect the best and, with God's help,
will attain the best."
Norman Vincent Peale

Demonstrating Our Love

*God is able to make every grace overflow to you,
so that in every way, always having everything you need,
you may excel in every good work.*
2 Corinthians 9:8 HCSB

How can we demonstrate our love for God? The Bible teaches us that obedience to Him is the surest sign of love (see 1 John 5:2).

In Ephesians 2:10 we read, "We are His workmanship, created in Christ Jesus for good works, which God prepared beforehand that we should walk in them" (NKJV). These words remind us that good works are an integral part of God's plan for our lives.

Today and every day, let the fruits of your life be a clear demonstration of your love for God. He has given you spiritual abundance and eternal life. All He asks in return is your faithfulness and your love.

*Hands are made for work,
and the heart is made for God.*
Josepha Rossello

The Rewards of Kindness

Kind people do themselves a favor,
but cruel people bring trouble on themselves.
Proverbs 11:17 NCV

Would you like an ironclad formula for improving your relationships, your attitude, and your life? Try this: Be kind to everybody. Don't just be kind to the people you know, or to the people who can help you, or to the "important" people you meet at work. Be kind to everyone you meet, with no exceptions. Strive to be kind even to those people who are not kind to you. Sometimes that's the toughest job of all.

But not surprisingly, kindness is its own reward. When you weave the thread of kindness into the fabric of your life, you'll be giving a priceless gift to others, and to yourself . . . but not necessarily in that order.

The happiness of life is
made up of minute fractions—the little,
soon-forgotten charities of a kiss or a smile,
a kind look or heartfelt compliment.
Samuel Taylor Coleridge

Real Wisdom

> Only the LORD gives wisdom;
> he gives knowledge and understanding.
> Proverbs 2:6 NCV

Genuine wisdom is found in the unique book that holds God's promises: the Bible. God's wisdom is unique because it renews not only the mind but also the heart. And the Bible makes promises upon which we can confidently depend.

Are you using your Bible as a tool for enlightenment and transformation? Do you consult God's Word every day, not just on Sunday mornings? And will you take God at His Word by trusting every single one of His promises? If so, you'll continue to grow spiritually, emotionally, and intellectually.

So make sure that God's Word is a bright spotlight that illuminates your path and guides your steps. It's the best way to live today, tomorrow, and every day of your life.

> *The essence of wisdom, from a practical standpoint, is*
> *pausing long enough to look at our lives—invitations,*
> *opportunities, relationships—from God's perspective.*
> *And then acting on it.*
> Charles Stanley

The Miracle Worker

Is anything impossible for the LORD?
Genesis 18:14 HCSB

God is a miracle worker. Throughout history He has intervened in the course of human events in ways that cannot be explained away by science or human rationale. And He's still doing so today.

God's miracles are not limited to special occasions, nor are they witnessed only by a select few. God is crafting His wonders all around us: the miracle of a newborn baby; of a world renewing itself with every sunrise; of lives transformed by God's love and grace. Each day God's handiwork is evident for all to see and experience.

Today, seize the opportunity to inspect God's hand at work. His miracles come in a variety of shapes and sizes, so keep your eyes and your heart open. Be watchful, and you'll be amazed.

I believe that God is in the miracle business—that His favorite way of working is to pick up where our human abilities and understandings leave off and then do something so wondrous and unexpected that there's no doubt who the God is around here.
Emilie Barnes

Being Patient with God's Timing

I wait for the LORD; I wait, and put my hope in His word.
Psalm 130:5 HCSB

As individuals, as families, as businesses, and as a nation, we are impatient for the changes we desire. We want solutions to our problems, and we want them right now. But sometimes life's greatest challenges defy easy—or quick—solutions, and so we must be patient.

Psalm 37:7 teaches us to "rest in the Lord, and wait patiently for Him" (NKJV). But for most of us, waiting patiently for God is difficult. Why? Because we usually demand solutions to our problems today, not tomorrow. We seek to manage our lives according to our own timetables, not God's. But instead of impatiently tapping our fingers, we should fold our fingers and pray. When we do, our heavenly Father will reward us in His own miraculous way and in His own perfect time.

We must leave it to God to answer our prayers
in His own wisest way. Sometimes, we are so impatient
and think that God does not answer.
God always answers! He never fails!
Be still. Abide in Him.
Mrs. Charles E. Cowman

The Only Lasting Peace

*Jesus himself stood in the midst of them,
and saith unto them, Peace be unto you.*
Luke 24:36 KJV

Peace can be a scarce commodity in our demanding, twenty-first-century world. After all, our culture is overflowing with an astounding array of distractions, interruptions, and temptations. How, then, can we find the peace we desire? By turning our days—and our lives—over to God.

Elisabeth Elliot wrote, "If my life is surrendered to God, all is well. Let me not grab it back, as though it were in peril in His hand but would be safer in mine!"

Are you willing to entrust your life to God? Will you build your life on the firm foundation of God's promises? If so, you'll experience the only peace that lasts: God's peace.

*God designed the human machine to run
on Himself. God cannot give us happiness
and peace apart from Himself,
because it is not there. There is no such thing.*
C. S. Lewis

Pleasing Everybody

Do you think I am trying to make people accept me?
No, God is the One I am trying to please.
Am I trying to please people? If I still wanted
to please people, I would not be a servant of Christ.
Galatians 1:10 NCV

If you're like most people, you're sensitive to rejection. But the fear of rejection can be a major roadblock on the path to a purposeful life. Why? Because the more fearful we are of displeasing others, the more likely we are to make decisions that are not in our best interest.

A far better strategy is to concentrate, first and foremost, on pleasing God. So today, focus your thoughts and energies on pleasing your Creator first and always. And when it comes to the world and all its inhabitants, don't worry too much about the folks you can't please. Focus, instead, on doing the right thing—and leave the rest up to God.

You must never sacrifice your relationship
with God for the sake of a relationship
with another person.
Charles Stanley

Hope and Purpose

The lines of purpose in your lives never grow slack,
tightly tied as they are to your future in heaven,
kept taut by hope.
Colossians 1:5 MSG

God has things He wants you to do and places He wants you to go, but sometimes His intentions will be unclear to you. At such times you may ask, "Where do You want me to go now, Lord? What do You want me to do next?"

If you earnestly seek God's will for your life, you will find it . . . in time. As you prayerfully consider God's path for your life, study the instructions in His Word and be ever watchful for His signs of direction in your life. And if your heavenly Father doesn't reveal Himself as quickly as you'd like, be patient and persevering, continually seeking His purpose for your life.

Rest assured, the lines of purpose in your life are there, and God knows every one. He intends to work in you and through you. He desires to lead you along a path of His choosing. Your challenge is to watch, to listen, and to follow Him wherever He leads.

Until your purpose lines up with God's purpose,
you will never be happy or fulfilled.
Charles Stanley

Overcoming Problems

People who do what is right may have many problems,
but the Lord will solve them all.
Psalm 34:19 NCV

In 1955, Rosa Parks rode a Montgomery, Alabama, bus into history. In those days, African Americans were required to give up their seats to whites. But Rosa refused—and so she was arrested. Her personal protest against injustice ignited the civil rights movement in the United States. Her philosophy was powerfully simple: "I don't waste too much time thinking about my problems. I just look around to see what I can do, and then I do it."

Difficult times call for courageous measures; but fear begets more fear, and anxiety is a poor counselor. So if you think you can't make changes in your world, think again. And while you're at it, remember Rosa Parks. Let her story inspire you, and then summon the courage to make big changes in your own life and in your world. Rosa did it, and so can you.

Conquering any difficulty always gives
one a secret joy, for it means pushing back
a boundary line and adding to one's liberty.
Henri Frédéric Amiel

A Word Aptly Spoken

*Kind words are like honey—sweet to the soul
and healthy for the body.*
Proverbs 16:24 NLT

The book of Proverbs offers much wisdom, and time and again it tells us that the words we speak can and should be beautiful offerings to those who hear them. But it also warns that our words can have unhappy consequences when we speak impulsively, thoughtlessly, or angrily.

Are you fully aware of the impact your words have on others? And as a consequence, do you measure your words carefully before you speak them? If so, you are wise—and those around you are blessed. But if you're like most people, you may, on occasion, speak before you think . . . and then have reason to regret your words.

Today, take control of your comments by engaging your mind before you rev up your vocal cords. After all, some things are better left unsaid . . . and you never have to apologize for thoughtless words you didn't speak.

In all your deeds and words, you should look on Jesus as your model, whether you are keeping silence or speaking, whether you are alone or with others.
Saint Bonaventure

Beyond Temptation

Jesus told him, "Go away, Satan! For it is written:
Worship the Lord your God, and serve only Him."
Matthew 4:10 HCSB

After fasting forty days and nights in the desert, Jesus was tempted by Satan. Christ used Scripture to rebuke the enemy (see Matthew 4:1–11), and we can and should do likewise. We must depend upon God's promises and use them to shield us from temptation.

We live in a world that is full of opportunities to stray from God's will. Ours is a society filled with distractions and temptations, a place where it's all too easy to disobey God. If we are to survive and prosper spiritually, we must be watchful; we must be faithful; and we must wrap ourselves in the protection of God's promises.

When we petition our Creator sincerely—and often—He will lead us away from the snares the enemy puts in our path. The Good Shepherd will lead us back to Himself. If we trust and follow Him, He will deliver us from evil, just as He has promised.

Our Lord has given us an example of how to overcome
the devil's temptations. When He was tempted in the
wilderness, He defeated Satan
every time by the use of the Bible.
Billy Graham

Financial Common Sense According to God

Follow the whole instruction the LORD your God has commanded you, so that you may live, prosper, and have a long life in the land you will possess.

Deuteronomy 5:33 HCSB

Countless books have been written about money— how to make it and how to keep it. But you probably already own at least one copy—and probably several copies—of the world's foremost guide to financial security. That book is the Bible. God's Word is not only a road map to eternal life; it's also an indispensable guidebook for life here on earth. As such, the Bible has much to say about life, faith, and finances.

God's Word promises that when we sow generously, we will reap generously (2 Corinthians 9:6). And the Bible promises that when we behave wisely, we'll be rewarded (Proverbs 16:20). So if you'd like to improve your finances (or any other aspect of your life), read God's instruction book—and follow it. When you do, you'll be blessed today, tomorrow, and every day of your life.

God's principles of finance are no longer on trial; they have held true over the years.

Larry Burkett

Faith for Tough Times

They cried out to the LORD in their trouble;
He saved them from their distress.
Psalm 107:13 HCSB

Life is a tapestry of good days and difficult days, but for most of us, if we're honest, the good days predominate. Yet it's during the good days, it seems, that we're tempted to take our blessings for granted. And it can be on life's difficult days that we discover precisely what we're made of. More importantly, we discover what our faith is made of.

Has your faith been put to the test? If so, then you know that with God's help, you can endure life's darker days. But if you have not yet faced notable trials and tragedies of life, brace yourself: you will. When those dark days come and your faith is put to the test, rest assured that God is perfectly able—and always ready—to give you strength for the struggle.

God has a bottle and a book for his people's tears.
What was sown as a tear will come up as a pearl.
Matthew Henry

God's Guidebook

*All Scripture is given by inspiration of God,
and is profitable for doctrine, for reproof, for correction,
for instruction in righteousness, that the man of God may
be complete, thoroughly equipped for every good work.*
2 Timothy 3:16–17 NKJV

God has given us a guidebook for life called the Bible. It contains thorough instructions which, if followed, will lead to fulfillment, spiritual abundance, and peace. The Creator has given us these instructions for the purpose of knowing Him: His power, His wisdom, His promises, and His love. As we study God's teachings and apply them to our lives, we live by the Word that will never pass away.

Today, make a promise to yourself and to your Creator: vow to follow His teachings and to conduct yourself in ways that make you a shining example of His love and righteousness to your friends, to your family, to your coworkers, and, most importantly, to those who have not yet discovered the timeless wisdom of God's Word.

Unless we form the habit of going to the Bible in bright moments as well as in trouble, we cannot fully respond to its consolations because we lack equilibrium between light and darkness.
Helen Keller

Unwelcome Changes

I have heard your prayer, I have seen your tears;
surely I will heal you.
2 Kings 20:5 NKJV

When life unfolds according to our wishes, or when we experience good fortune, we find it easy to praise God and to accept His plan. When change seems pleasing, we greet it with open arms. But sometimes the changes we must endure are painful. When we struggle through the more difficult days of life—when we face unwelcome changes, as we all must from time to time—we may ask, "Why me?"

The changes in our lives do have purpose . . . we just don't always understand what that purpose is. But God does. He is faithfully and lovingly working out His plan for your life.

Have you endured a difficult transition that has left your head spinning or your heart broken? If so, you have a choice to make: either you can frown and fret, or you can trust God. The former is a formula for disaster; the latter is a formula for a well-lived life.

If God has you in the palm of His hand and your real
life is secure in Him, then you can venture forth—into the
places and relationships,
the challenges, the very heart of the storm—
and you will be safe there.
Paula Rinehart

Obedience and Contentment

Praise the LORD! Happy are those who respect the LORD,
who want what he commands.
Psalm 112:1 NCV

Did you know that when we conduct ourselves in ways that are opposed to God's commandments, we rob ourselves of God's peace? When we give in to the temptations and distractions of our irreverent age, we rob ourselves of God's blessings. When we become preoccupied with material possessions or personal status, we forfeit the contentment that could be ours in Christ.

Where can we find the kind of contentment that God promises is available to each of us? Is it a result of wealth or power or fame? Hardly. Genuine contentment is a gift from God to those who follow His commandments and accept His plan. And it's a gift that must be discovered and rediscovered throughout life. It is a promise that we claim when we allow Christ to dwell at the center of our lives.

When we do what is right, we have contentment,
peace, and happiness.
Beverly LaHaye

Rewards of Discipline

*Apply your heart to discipline
and your ears to words of knowledge.*
Proverbs 23:12 NASB

God's Word reminds us again and again that our Creator expects us to lead disciplined lives. God doesn't reward laziness, misbehavior, or apathy. To the contrary, He expects those who follow Him to behave with dignity and discipline.

We live in a world in which leisure is glorified and indifference is often glamorized. But God did not create us for lives of mediocrity; He created us for far greater things.

Life's greatest rewards seldom fall into our laps; to the contrary, our greatest accomplishments usually require lots of work . . . which is exactly the way God planned it. After all, He knows that the rewards of discipline are well worth the effort.

The alternative to discipline is disaster.
Vance Havner

All the Energy You Need

Whatever you do, do it enthusiastically,
as something done for the Lord and not for men.
Colossians 3:23 HCSB

All of us suffer through trying times and difficult days. Fortunately, God offers us comfort and strength if we turn to Him.

Burning the candle at both ends is tempting but potentially destructive. Instead, we should put first things first and say no to the things we simply don't have the time or the energy to do. As we establish our priorities, we should turn to God and to His Word for guidance.

If you're a person with too many demands and too few hours in which to meet them, don't fret. Instead, focus on God and His love for you. Ask Him for the wisdom to prioritize your life and the strength to fulfill your responsibilities. God will give you the energy to do the most important things on today's to-do list if you put Him first. Then you can do whatever you do with enthusiasm and for the Lord.

Where there is much prayer, there will be much of the
Spirit; where there is much of the Spirit,
there will be ever-increasing power.
Andrew Murray

God's Protection

I know whom I have believed,
and am convinced that he is able to guard what
I have entrusted to him for that day.
2 Timothy 1:12 NIV

God promises that He will protect us (Psalm 121:8; Deuteronomy 31:8). Our job is to open ourselves to His protection and His love. When we do, we'll quickly discover that genuine faith—the kind of faith that allows us to trust God in every season of life—defeats fear.

The next time you find yourself facing a fear-provoking situation, ask yourself which is stronger: your faith or your fear. And before you answer that question, take time to reflect on God's promises for life here on earth *and* life eternal.

Your heavenly Father can manage every situation; He can solve every problem; and He can help you weather every storm. No challenge is too big for Him, not even yours. You can trust Him in every circumstance.

We can take great comfort that
God never sleeps—so we can.
Dianna Booher

Choosing Forgiveness

Blessed are the merciful,
because they will be shown mercy.
Matthew 5:7 HCSB

Forgiveness is a choice. We can either forgive those who have injured us, or we can hang on to past hurts. But when we allow bitterness and resentment to poison our hearts, we'll end up tortured because of our own shortsightedness. When we obey God by offering forgiveness to others, however, we'll be blessed.

Do you harbor resentment against anyone? If so, today you're faced with an important decision: whether to forgive the person who has hurt you. God's instructions in His Word and His example by His actions—forgiving us—are a clear communication that He wants us to forgive.

To forgive or not to forgive: that is the question. What will you answer?

Forgiveness is not an occasional act:
it is an attitude.
Martin Luther King Jr.

No Problem Too Big

God—His way is perfect; the word of the LORD is pure.
He is a shield to all who take refuge in Him.
Psalm 18:30 HCSB

In 1967, a diving accident left Joni Eareckson a quadriplegic. But she didn't give up. Unable to use her hands, she taught herself to paint fine art holding a brush between her teeth. Then the determined young woman began writing. To date, Joni Eareckson Tada has completed more than thirty books, and her ministry, Joni and Friends, touches the lives of millions.

Jesus said, "In this world you will have trouble. But take heart! I have overcome the world" (John 16:33 NIV). So the next time you face a difficult day or an unexpected challenge, remember Joni's journey. If she could meet her challenges with God's help, so can you. Take heart, trust the Father's promises, and remember that no problem is too big for God.

When considering the size of your problems,
there are two categories that you should never worry
about: the problems that are small enough
for you to handle and the ones that aren't
too big for God to handle.
Marie T. Freeman

No Fear

> *God has not given us a spirit of fearfulness,*
> *but one of power, love, and sound judgment.*
> *So don't be ashamed of the testimony about our Lord,*
> *or of me His prisoner. Instead, share in suffering for*
> *the gospel, relying on the power of God.*
> *2 Timothy 1:7–8 HCSB*

The Bible assures us that God is with us, so we can live courageously; but sometimes, here in the world of lightning-fast news cycles, it's hard to do. After all, we face an avalanche of negativity from a widening array of media sources that have discovered that bad news sells better than good. So headlines shout about shocking stories while good news often goes unreported.

Perhaps you, like so many others, have found your courage tested by the anxieties and fears that are an inevitable part of twenty-first-century life. If so, God wants to remind you that He is here, that He is strong, and that He loves you very much. So don't focus on your fears (or, for that matter, on the fears that big media want you to focus on). Instead, take your fears to Him . . . and leave them there.

Call upon God. Prayer itself can defuse fear.
Bill Hybels

December

A Grand Plan

I will instruct you and teach you in the way you should go;
I will guide you with My eye.
Psalm 32:8 NKJV

God has plans for your life that are grander than you can imagine. But God's plans may not always be clear to you. Sometimes the Father may lead you through the wilderness before He delivers you to the Promised Land. So be patient, keep praying, and keep seeking His will for your life. When you do, you'll be amazed at the marvelous things that an all-powerful, all-knowing God can do.

Are you determined to discover God's plan for your life? Are you willing to work, to pray, to watch, and to listen? If so, God's Word promises that He will lead you along a path of His choosing—and you can be sure that God's path is the perfect path for you.

God has a course mapped out for your life,
and all the inadequacies in the world will not change His
mind. He will be with you every step
of the way. And though it may take time,
He has a celebration planned for when you
cross over the "Red Seas" of your life.
Charles Swindoll

Still Growing

> *When I was a child, I spoke and thought*
> *and reasoned as a child. But when I grew up,*
> *I put away childish things.*
> 1 Corinthians 13:11 NLT

If we are to grow as individuals, we need both knowledge and wisdom. Knowledge is found in textbooks. Wisdom, on the other hand, is gained through experience, through years of trial and error, and through careful attention to the Word of God. Knowledge is an important building block in a well-lived life, and it pays rich dividends both personally and professionally. But wisdom is even more important because it shapes not only our minds but also our hearts.

When it comes to your faith, God doesn't intend for you to stand still. He wants you to keep growing as a human being and as a spiritual being. No matter how "grown-up" you may be, you still have more growing to do. And the more you grow, the more beautiful you become, inside and out.

> *One of the marks of spiritual maturity*
> *is a consistent, Spirit-controlled life.*
> Vonette Bright

Sharing the Joy

Let the hearts of those who seek the LORD rejoice.
Look to the LORD and his strength; seek his face always.
1 Chronicles 16:10–11 NIV

God's plan for us is that His joy should become our joy. He intends that we, His children, should share His love, His joy, and His peace. Yet sometimes, amid the hustle and bustle of living, we don't feel much like sharing anything, much less joy. So we forfeit God's gift as we wrestle with the challenges of everyday life.

If your heart is heavy today, open the door of your soul to your heavenly Father. When you do, He will renew your spirit. Then, look for ways to make your joy complete by sharing it. You'll discover that it's a wonderful way to say "I love you" to your family, to your friends, and especially to your God.

Joy is not the same as happiness—
although they may overlap.
Happiness depends on circumstances;
joy depends on God.
Billy Graham

Embracing God's Love

We love him, because he first loved us.
1 John 4:19 KJV

You know the profound love that you hold in your heart for your family and friends. As a child of God, you can only imagine the infinite love that your heavenly Father has for you.

Today, what will you do in response to God's love? Will you live purposefully and joyfully? Will you celebrate God's creation while giving thanks for His blessings? And will you share God's love with family members, friends, and even strangers? Hopefully so. After all, God's message—and His love—are meant to be shared.

Your heavenly Father—a God of infinite love and mercy—is waiting to embrace you with open arms. Accept His love, and share it, today . . . and forever.

When did God's love for you begin?
When He began to be God. When did He begin
to be God? Never, for He has always been
without beginning and without end,
and so He has always loved you from eternity.
Saint Francis de Sales

Obedience in Action

Obey God and be at peace with him;
this is the way to happiness.
Job 22:21 NCV

Obedience to God is measured not in words but in deeds. Talking rightly is easy; living rightly is far more difficult, especially in today's temptation-filled world.

Since God created Adam and Eve, we human beings have spent far too much time and far too much energy rebelling against our Creator. Why? Quite often it's because we are unwilling to trust God, to believe His Word, and to follow His commandments. But if we'll trust God, take His promises to heart, and follow His instructions carefully, deliberately, and consistently, we'll discover unsurpassed peace and joy.

God has promised to bless those who obey Him. Count yourself among that number today and every day. It's the guaranteed way to happiness.

Happiness is obedience,
and obedience is happiness.
C. H. Spurgeon

Meeting Expectations

*The person who knows my commandments
and keeps them, that's who loves me. And the person
who loves me will be loved by my Father,
and I will love him and make myself plain to him.*
John 14:21 MSG

Here's a quick quiz: whose expectations are you trying to meet?

A. Your friends' expectations

B. Society's expectations

C. God's expectations

If you're wise, you understand that the correct answer is C.

Far too many people invest far too much energy trying to meet others' expectations and far too little energy trying to please God. A smarter strategy would be to focus first on pleasing God. To do that, we must prioritize our days according to God's guidance (as found in His Word), and we must seek His will and His wisdom in all matters. Then we'll be able to face each day with the assurance that the same God who made the universe out of nothingness will help us make the right choices in life.

*Don't be addicted to approval. Follow your heart. Do
what you believe God is telling you to do,
and stand firm in Him and Him alone.*
Joyce Meyer

Beyond Denial

When the Spirit of truth comes,
he will lead you into all truth.
John 16:13 NCV

The words from the sixteenth chapter of John are straightforward—the Spirit of truth will lead us to truth. Yet we live in a world that allows and encourages us to avoid the truth (or to deny it altogether).

M. Scott Peck once said, "Truth or reality is avoided when it is painful. Mental health is an ongoing process of dedication to reality at all costs." And Dr. Peck was indeed correct: we're never completely healthy when we're in denial.

Today, as you fulfill the responsibilities that God has placed before you, ask yourself this question: "Do my thoughts and actions bear witness to the ultimate truth that God has placed in my heart, or am I allowing the pressures of everyday life to overwhelm me and draw me away from His truth?" Then ask God to lead you by His Spirit beyond denial to truth.

The single most important element in any human
relationship is honesty—with oneself,
with God, and with others.
Catherine Marshall

Forget or Regret

*Don't be wishing you were someplace else or with
someone else. Where you are right now is God's place
for you. Live and obey and love and believe right there.*
1 Corinthians 7:17 MSG

Bitterness can destroy you if you let it . . . so don't
let it!

If you are caught up in anger or regret, you know
all too well the destructive power of these emotions.
How can you rid yourself of them? First, prayerfully
ask God to free you from these feelings. Then, learn
to catch yourself whenever thoughts of bitterness
begin to creep into your mind. The goal is this: to
learn to resist negative thoughts before they hijack
your emotions.

So the next time you find yourself slipping into
the quicksand of regret, pull yourself out before you
get stuck. Do your best to keep your past in the past—
it's better to forget than regret.

*Bitterness is a spiritual cancer, a rapidly growing
malignancy that can consume your life.
Bitterness cannot be ignored but must be healed
at the very core, and only Christ can heal bitterness.*
Beth Moore

Finding Purpose Through Service

Prepare your minds for service and have self-control.
1 Peter 1:13 NCV

We achieve greatness through service to others. And every single day of your life, including this one, God will give you opportunities to serve Him by serving other people. Welcome those opportunities with open arms. Always be willing to pitch in and make the world a better place. Resist the temptation to keep all your blessings to yourself. When you share them, you'll earn rewards that are unavailable to folks who stubbornly refuse to serve.

Service is a character-building experience: the more you serve, the more you grow. So as you go about your daily activities, remember this: God's only Son made Himself a servant . . . and if you want to follow Him and know Him better, you'll do the same.

So long as we love we serve,
so long as we are loved by others,
I would almost say that we are indispensable;
and no man is useless while he has a friend.
Robert Louis Stevenson

The Source of Strength

*Don't you know who made everything? Haven't you
heard about him? The Lord is the God who lives forever.
He created everything on earth. He won't become worn
out or get tired. No one will ever know how great his
understanding is. He gives strength to those who are tired.
He gives power to those who are weak.*
Isaiah 40:28–29 NIrV

God is a never-ending source of power, and He
will give us courage if we call on Him. When
we're weary, He will give us strength. When we lose
hope, God will restore hope to our hearts. When
we grieve, God will wipe away our tears. These are
promises we can count on.

Do you feel overwhelmed by today's tasks? Do you
feel pressured by the ever-increasing demands of life?
Then turn your concerns and your fears over to God
in prayer. He knows your needs, and He has promised
to meet those needs. Whatever your circumstances,
God will provide, protect, guide, and care for you if
you let Him. Invite Him into your heart and allow
Him to renew your spirit today. Trust Him: He will
never fail you.

*We should talk to each other, but it's when we talk
together with God that we are fully strengthened.*
Annie Chapman

Using Your Time Wisely

Teach us to number our days,
that we may gain a heart of wisdom.
Psalm 90:12 NKJV

Time is a nonrenewable gift from God, but sometimes we treat our time here on earth as if it were not a gift at all. We may be tempted to fritter away too much time and energy in trivial pursuits and petty diversions. But our heavenly Father beckons each of us to a higher calling. God wants us to use our time wisely, to use it in accordance with His plan for our lives. And if we're wise, that's exactly what we'll want, too.

As you decide how you'll spend the time that's allotted to you today, this week, and throughout your life, remember that each new day is a special treasure to be savored . . . and used wisely. As a child of God, you have much to celebrate and much to do. It's up to you, and you alone, to honor your Creator for the gift of time by using that gift wisely.

Do you love life? Then do not squander time,
for that's the stuff life is made of.
Benjamin Franklin

Seeking God's Blessings

Commit everything you do to the LORD.
Trust him, and he will help you.
Psalm 37:5 NLT

When our dreams come true and our plans prove successful, we find it easy to thank our Creator and to trust His divine providence. But in times of sorrow or hardship, we may find ourselves questioning God's plan for our lives.

On occasion, you will confront circumstances that trouble you or even shake you to the very core of your soul. During these difficult days, you must find the wisdom and the courage to trust your heavenly Father despite your circumstances.

Are you a person who seeks God's blessings for yourself and your family? Then trust Him. Trust Him with your relationships. Trust Him with your priorities. Follow His instructions and pray for His guidance. Trust your heavenly Father day by day, moment by moment, in good times and in trying times. Then wait patiently for God's promised blessings . . . and prepare yourself for the joy and peace that will be yours when you do.

I trust completely in God, nothing else.
Joan of Arc

Perfect Wisdom

The wisdom of this world is foolishness in God's sight.
1 Corinthians 3:19 NIV

The world has its own brand of wisdom. Unfortunately, it's a brand of wisdom that's often wrong and sometimes dangerous. God, on the other hand, has His own brand of wisdom, and it's a wisdom that will never lead you astray.

Where will you place your trust today? Will you trust in the wisdom of fallible men and women, or will you place your faith in the wisdom of the infallible, all-knowing, loving God of the universe? How you answer that question will profoundly affect the course of your life.

Today, listen to the quiet voice of your heavenly Father—He is not a God of confusion. Talk with Him; listen to Him; trust Him. His perfect wisdom, unlike the "wisdom" of the world, will never let you down.

Because the world is deceptive, it is dangerous.
The world can even deceive God's own people
and lead them into trouble.
Warren Wiersbe

Not to Worry

Let not your heart be troubled; you believe in God,
believe also in Me.
John 14:1 NKJV

If you are like most people, you may, on occasion, find yourself worrying about health, about finances, about safety, about relationships, about family, and about countless other challenges of life, some great and some small.

Where is the best place to take your worries? Take them to God. Take your troubles to Him, and your fears, and your sorrows. Trust God's promise to heal your heart and guide your steps.

When you place your future—indeed your life—in God's hands, you can keep earthly troubles in proper perspective. And when you allow God's Word to guide your steps, you will eventually find the peace and spiritual abundance He has promised. Your challenge, then, is to worry less and to trust God more. It's the right way to think and the right way to live . . . today and every day.

Worry is the senseless process of cluttering up tomorrow's
opportunities with
leftover problems from today.
Barbara Johnson

Your Partnership with God

We are God's co-workers.
You are God's field, God's building.
1 Corinthians 3:9 HCSB

Do you seek a life of purpose and fulfillment? If so, the best way to realize that goal is to form a partnership with God.

You are God's work in progress. He wants to mold your heart and guide your steps, but because He created you as a creature of free will, He won't force you to follow His plan. That decision is yours alone. It's a series of decisions, really, because your answer comes in all the little (and big) choices you make each day. And your choices will be reflected in every step you take.

Today, as you meet the challenges of everyday life, strengthen your partnership with God through prayer, through obedience, through praise, through thanksgiving, and through service. God is the best possible partner, and He wants to be your partner in every aspect of life. It's an offer you won't want to turn down.

When you invite God to become your partner,
you invite untold blessings into your life.
Marie T. Freeman

Honoring God

I give my final advice:
Honor God and obey his commands.
Ecclesiastes 12:13 NCV

Whom will you choose to honor today? If you choose to honor God and place Him at the center of your life, this day—and every day—will be a cause for celebration. But sometimes you may not feel like celebrating anything, not even God's blessings.

When the demands of life leave you rushing with scarcely a moment to spare, it's easy to forget to thank God for the gifts He has bestowed upon you. But do your best not to let that happen, because the one who loses out is you. Focusing on our problems, or even just on our work, can bring us down. But when we take a time-out to meditate on God's promises and our blessings, our spirits will be elevated and we'll find renewed strength and energy.

When you put God first and honor Him every day, on good days and bad, He will honor your efforts by providing all you need.

The greatest honor we can give Almighty God is to live
gladly because of the knowledge of His love.
Juliana of Norwich

Whose Values?

*I pray this: that your love will keep on growing in
knowledge and every kind of discernment,
so that you can determine what really matters.*
Philippians 1:9–10 HCSB

From the time your alarm clock wakes you in the morning until the moment you lay your head on the pillow at night, your actions are guided by the values you hold most dear. And if you want to experience God's blessings, you'll make sure that your values are shaped by His promises.

Society seeks to impose its own set of values on you and your family, but often, these values are contrary to God's Word (and thus contrary to your best interests). The world promises happiness, contentment, prosperity, and abundance. But genuine abundance is not a by-product of worldly possessions or status; it is a by-product of your thoughts, your actions, and your relationship with the Creator.

The world's promises are incomplete and deceptive; God's promises are unfailing. Your challenge, then, is to build your value system upon the one that never fails: God's value system.

*Having values keeps a person focused
on the important things.*
John Maxwell

Beyond Envy

*Rid yourselves of all wickedness,
all deceit, hypocrisy, envy, and all slander.*
1 Peter 2:1 HCSB

The Bible tells us to rid ourselves of envy, but in a competitive, cutthroat world, it's easy to become envious of others' success. We know that envy is wrong, but because we are frail, imperfect human beings, we may find ourselves struggling with feelings of envy or resentment—or both. These may be especially forceful when we see other people experience unusually good fortune.

Have you recently felt the pangs of envy creeping into your heart? If so, it's time to shift your focus to the marvelous things God has done for you and your family. And just as importantly, do your best to shift your focus away from the gifts God has chosen to give others.

Want a surefire formula for a happier, healthier life? Count your own blessings, and let your neighbors count theirs. When you do, you'll move beyond envy to joy and contentment.

*As a moth gnaws a garment,
so does envy consume a man.*
Saint John Chrysostom

Each Day a Gift

On your feet now—applaud God!
Bring a gift of laughter, sing yourselves into his presence.
Psalm 100:1–2 MSG

Life should never be taken for granted. Each day is a priceless gift from God and should be treated as such. Yet at times, because we get busy with too many tasks and have too little time to complete them, we may not slow down long enough to thank the Giver of all the good things we enjoy. When we allow ourselves to become that busy, too preoccupied to praise God, we cheat ourselves and our loved ones out of the blessing of joy.

Today, as the sun peaks over the horizon, let it remind you that you have one more reason—this glorious new day—to celebrate life. Will you treat today as a priceless treasure, a unique opportunity to follow God and enjoy His creation? Come on, get on your feet and applaud God. Laugh! Sing as you enter His presence—and remain in His presence, thankfully and joyfully, today and always.

The time for universal praise is sure to come someday.
Let us begin to do our part now.
Hannah Whitall Smith

Three Voices

*Those who live only to satisfy their own sinful nature
will harvest decay and death from that sinful nature.
But those who live to please the Spirit will harvest
everlasting life from the Spirit.*
Galatians 6:8 NLT

Every time you face an important decision, you'll
likely hear advice from three distinct voices. One
is the quiet voice of God's Spirit, informing your
conscience and directing you toward what's right.

Another voice you'll hear—a voice that is
sometimes quiet and sometimes not—is the voice
of temptation. It urges you to do what's selfish,
expedient, harmful, or just plain wrong. The voice of
temptation is definitely not from God.

The final voice you will hear is your own: the
voice that renders your decision as to which of the
first two voices you'll listen to.

Today, you'll choose between right and wrong,
between wisdom and foolishness, between rationality
and impulsivity. Before you make your decision,
listen carefully to the voice of God in your heart. His
voice will never lead you astray.

*Christian joy is a gift from God
flowing from a good conscience.*
Saint Philip Neri

Your Daily Journey

He maketh me to lie down in green pastures:
he leadeth me beside the still waters. He restoreth my soul.
Psalm 23:2–3 KJV

Even the most inspired folks can, from time to time, find themselves running on empty. The inevitable demands of daily life can drain us of our strength and rob us of the joy God promises and that He wants us to experience. But there's good news: the Father stands ready to renew our spirits, even on the darkest of days. God's Word tells us that when we lift our hearts and prayers to Him, He will restore our souls.

This day provides yet another opportunity to praise God, to talk to Him, and to walk with Him. When you do these things, your heavenly Father will guide you and protect you. So today, as you encounter the obligations and opportunities of everyday life, make sure that you've opened your heart to the Creator. When you do, He'll give you the wisdom and the strength to meet any challenge.

Walking with God leads to receiving
His intimate counsel,
and counseling leads to deep restoration.
John Eldredge

Coming Alongside

*He comes alongside us when we go through hard times,
and before you know it, he brings us alongside
someone else who is going through hard times
so that we can be there for that person
just as God was there for us.*
2 Corinthians 1:4 MSG

Do you delight in the victories of others? You should. Each day provides countless opportunities to encourage others and to commend their good works. When you do, you spread seeds of joy and happiness . . . and that's precisely what God wants you to do.

So make this promise to yourself, to God, and—even if it's not verbalized—to your fellowman: Vow to be a source of encouragement to everyone you meet. Keep a smile on your face and kind words on your lips. It may be exactly why God has brought certain people alongside you.

*A single word,
if spoken in a friendly spirit,
may be sufficient to turn one from dangerous error.*
Fanny Crosby

Faith That Works

*In the same way faith, if it doesn't have works,
is dead by itself.*
James 2:17 HCSB

The central message of the apostle James's letter is the need for followers of God to act upon their beliefs. James's instruction is clear: faith without works is dead. God's Word teaches that we are redeemed by our faith in Christ, but salvation does not signal the end of our earthly responsibilities; it marks the beginning of our work for the Lord.

If your faith in God is strong, you will find yourself drawn toward God's work. You'll serve Him not just with words or prayers but also with deeds. Because of your faith in God, you'll feel compelled to do God's work—to do it gladly, faithfully, joyfully, and consistently.

Today, redouble your efforts to do God's bidding here on earth. Never have the needs—or the opportunities—been greater.

*Where there are no good works, there is no faith. If works
and love do not blossom forth, it is not genuine faith, the
Gospel has not yet gained
a foothold, and Christ is not yet rightly known.*
Martin Luther

What the Heart Knows

*They show that in their hearts they know
what is right and wrong.*
Romans 2:15 NCV

In times of crisis it's especially hard to trust our own instincts, because our inner voice—our conscience or intuition—can be drowned out by fear, worry, anxiety, or confusion. That's why, in such times, we must do whatever it takes to look deep within our own hearts, where—if we're sensitive to God's Spirit— we usually do know right from wrong. Our best, and hopefully most trusted, adviser is the Spirit's quiet voice. And it's up to us to listen carefully, even when our world seems filled with noise and static.

Are you facing an important decision? Pray about it and listen quietly to God's whispering deep within your heart. When you listen to Him, you can be certain that the answer will be the right one for you.

*In the soul-searching of our lives,
we are to stay quiet so we can hear Him say
all that He wants to say to us in our hearts.*
Charles Swindoll

Your Bright Future

> *I know the thoughts that I think toward you,*
> *says the LORD, thoughts of peace and not of evil, to give*
> *you a future and a hope. Then you will call upon Me*
> *and go and pray to Me, and I will listen to you.*
> Jeremiah 29:11–12 NKJV

How bright is your future? The answer, if you trust God's promises, is that your future is very bright indeed!

But here's a slightly different question: how bright do you believe your future to be? Are you anticipating a terrific tomorrow, or are you dreading a terrible one? Your answer is important, because your outlook and expectation will have a powerful impact on the way tomorrow turns out.

Corrie ten Boom offered this advice: "Never be afraid to trust an unknown future to a known God." And it's advice all of us should take to heart. God has good plans for each of us, including you. So trust His promises, look forward to a bright future . . . and get to work building a better today.

> *It may be that the day of judgment will dawn tomorrow;*
> *in that case, we shall gladly stop working*
> *for a better tomorrow. But not before.*
> Dietrich Bonhoeffer

The Gift of Laughter

Clap your hands, all you nations;
shout to God with cries of joy.
Psalm 47:1 NIV

Laughter is a gift from God; and as with every gift from His hand, it's one He intends for us to use. Yet sometimes we get bogged down in the stress of everyday living, and we fail to find the fun in life. When we allow life's inevitable disappointments to cast a pall over our lives and our souls, we cheat ourselves and our loved ones out of the joy God wants us all to experience.

Because of God's great love for us, we have ample reason to be cheerful and to be thankful. He has blessed us beyond measure, starting with the inexpressibly wonderful gift that is ours for the asking: eternal life.

So today, as you go about your daily activities, approach life with good cheer, with a smile, and even with a chuckle. After all, God created laughter for a reason . . . so laugh!

Laughter is a tranquilizer with no side effects.
Arnold H. Glasgow

Finding God's Love

*He has not stopped showing his kindness
to the living and the dead.*
Ruth 2:20 NIV

Where can we find God's love? Everywhere. God's love transcends space and time. It reaches beyond the heavens, and it touches the darkest, smallest corner of every human heart. When we sincerely open our minds and hearts to God, He will fill them to overflowing with His infinite love.

Joyce Meyer said, "God has the marvelous ability to love us in the midst of our imperfections." And if He can love us unconditionally, surely we can find the wisdom and the courage to accept His love.

Today, thank God for His never-ending kindness and welcome His love into your heart. When you do, His transcendent love will surround you and transform you.

*A joyful heart is like a sunshine of God's love,
the hope of eternal happiness,
a burning flame of God. . . . And if we pray,
we will become that sunshine of God's love—
in our own home, the place where we live,
and in the world at large.*
Mother Teresa

Stuck?

GOD, *your God, is above all a compassionate God.*
In the end he will not abandon you,
he won't bring you to ruin, he won't forget the covenant
with your ancestors which he swore to them.
Deuteronomy 4:30–31 MSG

God loves you, and He wants to lead you to a place of abundance and joy. But on some days joy may seem only a distant, unfulfilled promise. Sometimes you may feel trapped by circumstances that are beyond your control. If today is one of those days, today is also the day to turn things over to God. Are you facing a situation that seems hopeless? With God, there's always hope. Do you feel stuck in a place that's uncomfortable for you? God is as near as your next breath, and He's capable of delivering you—or seeing you through victoriously.

Your road may not be easy or smooth, but God never promised ease. He promised to walk with you, to give you strength, and to never leave you. And He promises that what He provides will always be sufficient to meet your needs.

God promises us a safe landing, not smooth sailing.
Anonymous

When Bad Things Happen

Now we see indistinctly, as in a mirror,
but then face to face. Now I know in part,
but then I will know fully, as I am fully known.
1 Corinthians 13:12 HCSB

God has a plan for our world and for our lives—He does not do things by accident. God is willful and intentional, yet we cannot always understand His purposes. Why? Because we are mortal beings with limited understanding. And although we cannot fully comprehend, we can always trust the will of God.

Sometimes we are touched by circumstances, the reasons for which we cannot comprehend. But of this we can be certain: God does comprehend. In the midst of chaos, He remains steadfast; in the midst of tragedy, He remains a pillar of strength. In the midst of our own confusion, His promises—and His love—remain unchanged. So we must turn our fears and doubts over to Him.

When terrible things happen, there are two choices,
and only two: We can trust God, or we can defy Him.
We believe that God is God, He's still got the whole world
in His hands and knows exactly what He's doing,
or we must believe that He is not God
and that we are at the awful mercy of mere chance.
Elisabeth Elliot

Eternally Grateful
and Exceedingly Humble

God is against the proud, but he gives grace to the humble.
1 Peter 5:5 NCV

God's Word indicates clearly and often that we should be humble. And those passages are good reminders, because as fallible human beings, we have a fair amount to be humble about. But the point of being humble isn't to feel bad about ourselves; it's simply to view ourselves realistically in light of God's perfection. None of us is perfect . . . we're not even close. When we're honest with ourselves and with God, we'll find that we simply can't be boastful; but we will be exceedingly humble. And when we remember that God promises to bless the humble, we'll also be eternally grateful.

The good things in our lives, including our loved ones, come from God. He deserves the glory, and in truth it's a glorious experience when we give it to Him.

So today, stay humble. It's the intellectually honest way to live . . . and it opens the way for God to fill your life with grace.

The preoccupation with self is
the enemy of humility.
Franklin Graham

Heeding the Call

I, therefore, the prisoner in the Lord,
urge you to walk worthy of the calling you have received.
Ephesians 4:1 HCSB

Do you know that it's vitally important for you to heed God's calling by discovering and developing your talents and your spiritual gifts? If you desire to make a difference—and if you seek to leave a worthy legacy to generations yet unborn—you must discover your gifts and begin using them for God's glory.

Every person has a unique set of talents and opportunities. Have you found your special calling? If so, congratulations—and keep up the good work. If not, keep searching and keep praying until you find out what it is that God wants you to do with your life. He has important work for you, and the time to begin that work is now.

The place where God calls you
is the place where your deep gladness
and the world's deep hunger meet.
Frederick Buechner

Notes

These pages have been provided
for your personal journaling and meditation.

Notes

Notes

Notes

Notes

Notes

Notes

Also available in the
Hugs Daily Inspirations
series . . .

Hugs Daily Inspirations for Women
Hugs Daily Inspirations, Words of Comfort
Hugs Daily Inspirations for Moms

HOWARD BOOKS
A DIVISION OF SIMON & SCHUSTER

Scripture References